CHILDREN OF THE DRAGON

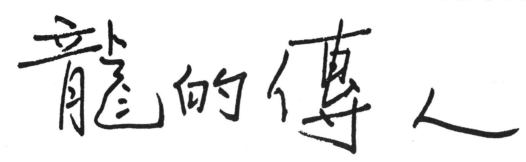

龍的傳人

方勵之

CHILDREN OF

Kenneth Jarecke (Contact Press Images)

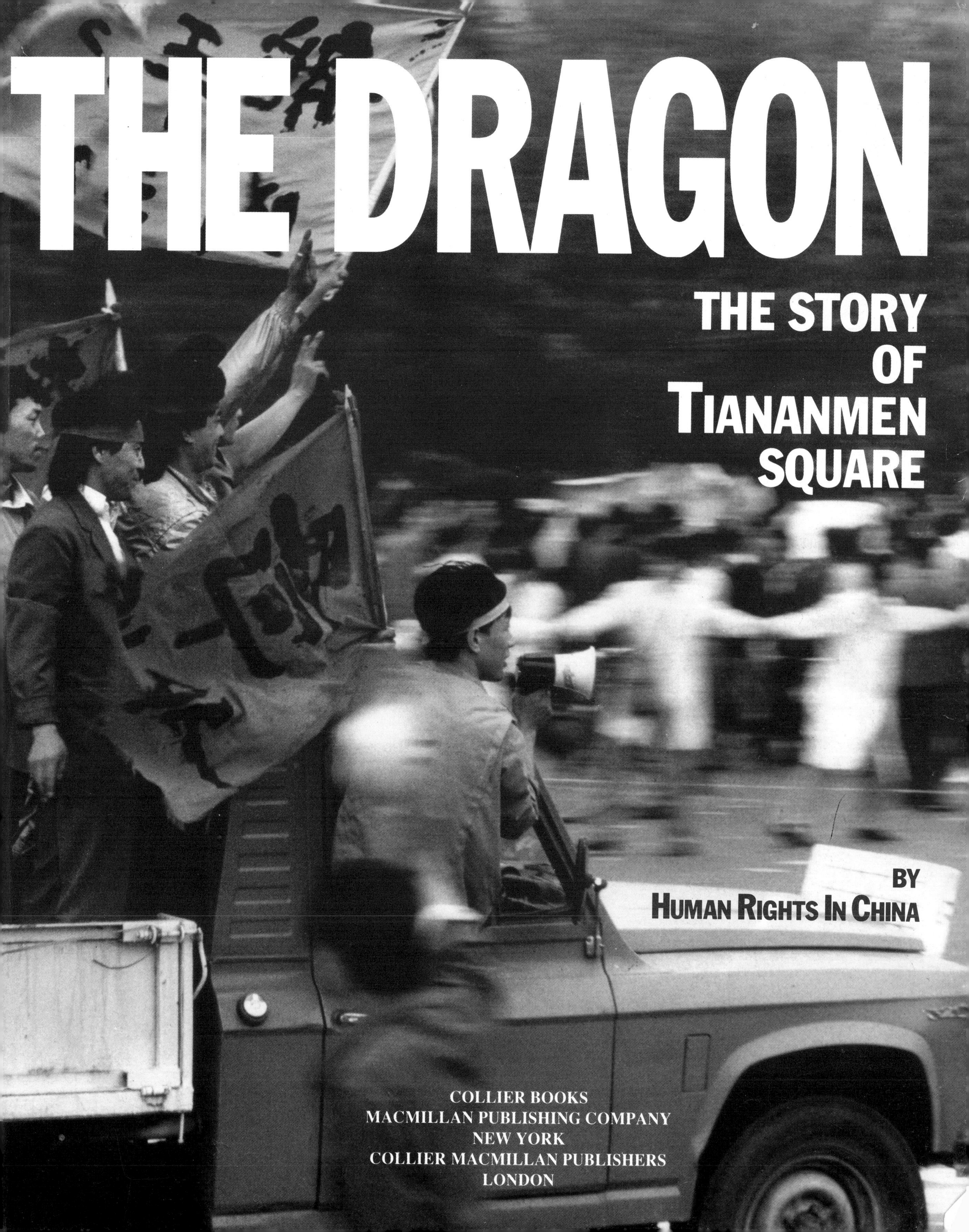

THE DRAGON

THE STORY OF TIANANMEN SQUARE

BY
HUMAN RIGHTS IN CHINA

COLLIER BOOKS
MACMILLAN PUBLISHING COMPANY
NEW YORK
COLLIER MACMILLAN PUBLISHERS
LONDON

Collier Books
Macmillan Publishing Company
866 Third Avenue, New York,
NY 10022
Collier Macmillan Canada, Inc.

Library of Congress
Cataloging-in-Publication Data
Children of the Dragon: The Story
of Tiananmen Square by Human
    Rights in China, Inc.
        p.   cm.
    ISBN 0-02-033520-2
    1. China—History—Tiananmen
    Square Incident, 1989. I. Human
    Rights in China, Inc. (Organization)
    DS779.32.C47   1989
    951'.156058—dc20
    89-49544   CIP

Macmillan books are available
at special discounts for bulk
purchases for sales promotions,
premiums, fund-raising, or
educational use.
For details, contact:
    Special Sales Director
    Macmillan Publishing Company
    866 Third Avenue
    New York, NY 10022

Design by Robert Pledge
Half-title page calligraphy by Fang Lizhi

10 9 8 7 6 5 4 3 2

Printed in the
United States of America

This book is dedicated to all those
who died during the tragedy of spring 1989.

CONTENTS

Students support the hunger strike.
Erica Lansner (Black Star)

PREFACE

by John K. Fairbank

The renascence of democracy failed in China in the spring of 1989 but succeeded dramatically in Eastern Europe later in the year. The crackdown at Tiananmen Square on June 4 was viewed around the world as a disaster for China. Perhaps its negative example helped deter repression in Eastern Europe. But how does June 4 fit into history? Behind China's Communist Party dictatorship stretched 3,000 years of imperial autocracy. And behind the students marching for democracy lay the ancient tradition of scholar candidates awaiting appointment to the imperial bureaucracy. Although the ingredients of student protest and public demonstration in April and June of 1989 superficially resembled their counterparts in Eastern Europe, they were rooted deeply within China's unique political tradition.

Down to the twentieth century China's rulers shared with their civil servants the ideology of imperial Confucianism, which enjoined every student to study the classics, revere the ancestors and the emperor, and to obey his officials. The emperor himself, studying the same classics, performed the duties that would keep the system working and in balance. These duties included the summary execution of all traitors who opposed the imperial power, or simply his policies.

By 1989 that shared ideology had been discredited and displaced by ideas from abroad as well as by the evolution of political thought and practices within China. China's new Communist rulers learned to use Marxism-Leninism to organize the quest for power and to advance industrialization once power had been achieved. On the other hand, the successors to the Confucian scholar class had proliferated into a whole panoply of new kinds of professional people, scientists, humanists, and technocrats; liberated from Confucianism, they created a new literature, inaugurated the social sciences, and modernized China's intellectual world.

Mao, however, found these intellectuals too familiar with the non-Communist West, and too professional to be easily coerced: in short, too unreliable for his narrow purposes of control. Deng Xiaoping, in turn, found them essential for modernization, but still incapable of intellectual subservience to the party. During the 1980s a precarious balance was maintained while economic growth went ahead without substantial political reform.

As the strains of modernization intensified, the problem of political reform grew critical. At first, in their confrontation at Tiananmen, both the rulers and their civil-servants-to-be in the universities followed certain traditional patterns of conduct. The students passively petitioned their rulers to address their problems and to allow them to take part in politics. The rulers reasserted their mandate to monopolize the direction of China's progress and prevent at all costs her falling into the "chaos" of unplanned activity and disharmony. They were unable to face the fact that, as Eastern Europe has now shown us, modern government requires popular participation in policy making.

Only the small intellectual elite had independent views of the potentialities of political reform, and they were deeply frustrated. The most insidious aspect of this frustration lay in the fact that the intellectuals were inhibited partly by the lingering influence of China's old order in their own thinking. Many felt an instinctive respect for government authority and believed that official permission was necessary before they could take any action on their own. To be Chinese and to be modern demands the creation of a new Chinese politics different both from China's past and from examples in the outside world. It is a hard and unenviable task, and still uncompleted after almost a century.

The crackdown of June 4 has now marked a turning point in which patriots both within China and abroad have a chance to consider anew China's future politics. Western observers can only sympathize with this arduous effort and try to assist from the sidelines. In doing so, we can find inspiration in the eyewitness accounts and photographs included in this volume.

Tiananmen Square.
Mark Avery (AP)

INTRODUCTION

by Orville Schell

To stand, in May 1989, atop the Gate of Heavenly Peace, which guards the southern entrance to the Forbidden City, and look out across the vast crowd of people jammed into Tiananmen Square was to have a historically new sense of what Mao called "the broad masses." It was to this ancient gate that Mao himself came on October 1, 1949, almost forty years before, to greet the adoring "broad masses" upon the defeat of the Nationalists of Chiang Kai-shek and the founding of "New China." Just the day before, in a declaration for the first plenary session of the Chinese People's Political Consultative Conference, he had proclaimed: "We are holding this session at a time when the Chinese people have triumphed over their enemies, changed the face of their country and founded the People's Republic of China. We the 475 million Chinese people have now stood up, and the future of our nation is infinitely bright."

It was to be a new beginning, which, for many Chinese, promised the hope of delivering their country from the warfare, corruption, economic ruin, and seemingly endless and humiliating failures that had plagued its history for so long. Through the selfless devotion of its people to socialism and country, Mao promised that China would be uplifted from its status as the "sick man of Asia." He went on in his declaration to proclaim defiantly that his new government would "organize the overwhelming majority of the Chinese people in political, military, economic, cultural, and other organizations and put an end to the old China, so that the great collective strength of the masses may be tapped both to support the people's Government and the People's Liberation Army and to build a new China, independent, democratic, peaceful, unified, prosperous, and strong."

During the spring of 1989, Mao's dream for China seemed far away indeed. Not only had most of the main principles of his revolution been annulled by recent reforms, but Tiananmen Square itself was filled with hundreds of thousands of dissident free-thinkers deriding the very party Mao had helped found and challenging the very notion of the "dictatorship of the proletariat." Moreover, instead of marching in lockstep from a single direction with resolute Socialist smiles as they had done in the past, people now spilled helter-skelter down the Avenue of Eternal Peace from both east and west, where, with flying banners extolling bourgeois democracy, they converged chaotically in the square, and then swirled and eddied like two turbulent rivers in a confluence. Even in the back alleys and surrounding neighborhoods of the city, one could hear their clamor reverberating like the roar from a faraway cataract.

This historic upheaval started in mid-April with the death of former Party chief Hu Yaobang, who had been accused of being too liberal in his treatment of intellectuals and students, and who was unceremoniously dismissed by Deng Xiaoping in January 1987 shortly after the last demonstrations for democracy—relatively mild ones involving perhaps 50,000 people—had shaken China. This time a group of students from several schools of higher education in Beijing, particularly Beijing University and Beijing Normal University, seized on Hu's death as the symbolic moment to vent their long pent-up dissatisfaction with the slowness of political reform, the lack of freedom of expression in China, and the endemic corruption that had riddled the Party and government. When they marched on Tiananmen Square to mark Hu's passing, they were joined by thousands of other young people. If nothing more had happened, this one demonstration against the Deng regime would have been a historic event. But the students did not stop here.

On April 26, after several more demonstrations, the new student movement faced its first direct challenge from the government when it was attacked by an editorial in the official Party paper, *People's Daily.* The editorial called the protests an "organized conspiracy to sow chaos" led by "people with ulterior motives," whose purpose was "to poison minds, create national turmoil, and sabotage the nation's political stability." In response, some 150,000 angry students defied the government and, after several tense confrontations, succeeded in breaking through police lines and reaching Tiananmen Square once more.

What was so striking about this triumphant march was that all along their route the students were greeted by onlookers who not only cheered them but gave them food and drink. Never had the capital seen such a bold public outpouring of support for political opposition. Then, on May 4, the anniversary of the May 4 Movement of 1919, when China's first student protests erupted, there was another march, this time drawing more than 100,000 students.

After a brief lull, when it looked as if the situation might quiet down, the students decided on a bold new plan. In anticipation of Mikhail Gorbachev's visit on May 15, about 1,000 students entered the square at night to begin a hunger strike. From that day until the bloody finale on June 4, Tiananmen Square, the symbolic heart of the capital and the country, became a nonstop theater of mass contention. The crowds that immediately began gathering to support the fasting students would have been beyond the imagining of Mao, who built the one-hundred-acre square for rituals of loyalty, not dissent. These latter-day activists wore everything from acid-washed jeans to three-piece suits and neckties, from T-shirts inscribed with the words "Science and Democracy" to short skirts. With each passing day the number of protesters and onlookers grew in size and social diversity until, by the third week in May, the crowd became one of the largest and most representative bodies of urban Chinese society ever to assemble in one place.

Talking to student protesters during the early days of the protest one had little sense of them as intractable revolutionaries bent on deposing the government or Party, or even of their having unappeasable resentments toward the leadership. All this was yet to come. What was most noticeable about them at this time was their yearning to be listened to and to be taken seriously by their government as constructive and patriotic. Student representatives even kneeled on the steps of the Great Hall of the People and bowed their heads in supplication. More familiar with the kind of hostile student protester who views his government and police as unalterable enemies, Western reporters were often startled and even sometimes touched by the sense of sweetness and earnestness that they found among these Chinese students. Many had even made out their wills, not so much because they wished for apocalypse but to express their willingness to sacrifice all for principle, in the face of political adversity.

L i Peng and Deng and most of the other hard-line Party leaders seemed incapable of understanding that the students, had touched a nerve of disaffection with the Party and government that ran deeply through almost all levels of Chinese society. Intellectuals were frustrated by the slow pace of political reform, their dismally low salaries, and restrictions on publishing and travel. Workers on fixed incomes were angry at the way their buying power had been reduced by inflation (which had been running at well over 30 percent). Students were fed up not only with their lack of freedom but with squalid living conditions, dull curricula, and the government's refusal to make adequate investments in education. And scholars returning from abroad were dispirited to find that older cadres, more interested in protecting their positions and saving face than in modernizing and developing China, all too often discriminated against them and their newly acquired Western skills.

Young people were angry at being assigned to dead-end jobs or being left without jobs at all. Engineers, doctors, economists, teachers, and other professionals who still worked for the state were distressed to see their counterparts in private enterprise earning ten, sometimes twenty times more than they. And virtually everybody was fed up with the rampant corruption, nepotism, and favoritism that had invaded all branches of government.

B y Monday, May 15, students began flooding into the square, and a kindling point of sorts was reached. By Tuesday, more and more groups of intellectuals, journalists, and teachers had joined in. By Wednesday, hotel employees, hospital nurses, middle- and grade-school students, and even groups from China's national airline, the Foreign Ministry, the police, and the Party's school for cadres had begun to appear. And by Thursday, bus and taxi drivers, employees from the state railroad and the huge Capital Iron and Steel Works, factory and construction workers, even night soil collectors and peasants from the outskirts began to pour into the city and career with reckless abandon through the streets of Beijing in commandeered trucks and buses. To observers, it seemed as if the government had lost control of the capital. Moreover, news reports claimed that the protest had spread to almost every major city in China, causing an almost millennarian sense among the swarms of people in the streets. It was even reported that *liumang,* or hooligans, had gotten together and agreed to stop their petty thievery in favor of working with the students by helping to direct traffic and collect food. Never, in fifteen years of visiting Beijing, had I seen so many people smiling as I now saw in Tiananmen Square.

But the ebullience also created a strangely unreal atmosphere in which some of the protesters seemed tempted to believe that nothing could hurt them now. One young man only half-jokingly told me, "We are like the Boxers of 1900. We believe that not even bullets can pierce us!" In this self-contained universe where one could read political leaflets denouncing the Party, or listen to political speeches—in which the leadership was reviled as hopelessly corrupt and incompetent—with impunity, it was hard even to imagine the outside world much less a military crackdown.

Having avoided the violence and brutality that was inflicted on so many of the previous generation during the Cultural Revolution, the peaceful hunger strike was a hopeful, if curious, break with China's long history of politics through brute force. Not one single person died before the troops entered after the declaration of martial law on May 20. The infectious sense of elation and invulnerability came, I think, from the recognition that something historic and completely new was happening in China. This gave the protesters a sense of self-confidence and invincibility that later infused ordinary citizens with the courage and conviction to sit down in front of armored vehicles, and even to stand their ground against troops firing live ammunition. The word "*shengyuan,*" or support, was written almost everywhere one looked—on people's banners, headbands, clothing, the sides of cars, ambulances, buses, and trucks.

What was unprecedented about the movement was that the Chinese had stood up in such numbers to oppose a discredited vision that China's old-guard revolutionaries still proclaimed was meaningful and workable. Party leaders, who for so many years had been able to count on the people to obey and follow them out of respect, were no longer certain that the people would even follow them out of fear.

On May 18, just two days before martial law was declared, I went down to the square one last time before leaving Beijing. Standing on the back of a bicycle cart, just in front of the enormous portrait of Mao that hangs on the northern side of Tiananmen Square, I watched while hundreds of thousands of newly arrived demonstrators surged down the Avenue of Eternal Peace, many of them students who had just come from the train station after traveling to the capital from remote parts of China. It seemed incontrovertible to me that even if the government was somehow able to banish the million-odd demonstrators pressing, chanting, and singing around me, and even if Deng and his allies in the Party could succeed in holding on to their official positions of power, China would never be the same again.

Something fundamental between the Chinese Communist Party (CCP) and the people it purported to represent had broken. In the minds of most politically conscious Chinese, China had again entered the final stage of decline that had marked the end of so many dynasties before this one. Even before the final massacre on June 4, utter cynicism had replaced any lingering belief in the right of the Chinese Communist Party to rule, so that when it came to that bloody night, as horrible as it was, it represented only the final coup de grace of the Party's legitimacy. After these weeks, few Chinese who had participated in these events or who had even seen them on Chinese television (which was uncensored for the first time in forty years) would ever be able to look on the Party or Chinese politics in the same light. Too many people from too many walks of life had felt the headiness of challenging unjust authority.

But there was another, even more important, aspect to the events of last spring. They seemed to fill many Chinese with a new sense of accomplishment and pride. China had attracted the admiring attention of the entire world, and by so doing had succeeded in reinstating itself as a place of world significance. As student leader Wuer Kaixi later told me, "This was the first time that we Chinese were able to feel proud of being Chinese, that we were able to respect ourselves as equal to other people in the world."

Thus the accomplishment of the Tiananmen protest was not only that it changed the existing relationship between the Chinese people and their government, but that it altered the chemistry of the way they, particularly the younger generation of Chinese, looked at themselves. By taking to the streets, the Chinese had declared to be over their days of waiting compliantly for Party reform from the top. Through their defiance, large segments of Chinese urban society gained a tantalizing taste of what it felt like to be truly "liberated." For China's out-of-touch leaders, who talked of "Socialist democracy" but viewed the idea as either a tactical device to create the mere appearance of democratization or a ploy to stimulate economic energy and reform, the significance of this new liberation was difficult to comprehend. Infuriated at being humiliated by their own people in front of both Gorbachev and the world, and angered by the way in which the mystique of their once seemingly omnipotent rule had been punctured by their once compliant subjects, they turned to their time-tested tactic of a crackdown. What they were incapable of realizing, however, was that, after the events of spring, such tactics would never again be as completely effective as they once were. Not only did a crackdown fail to address the deep-seated grievances that had caused the uprising, but having experienced these few exhilarating weeks of freedom, the Chinese people would be less willing than ever to submit to new Party demands for obedience. They might appear to be conforming to Party dictates, but it seems likely that inside they will remain in a state of rebellion. The repression succeeded only in antagonizing the people further, in stifling the kind of imagination and energy on which China's future development depends.

In the end, it seems likely that future disaffection will be expressed more in economic demands than in political ones as China's faltering economy continues to flag. Economic problems that existed before the spring of 1989 will now be magnified many times over as people express their discontent through work slow-downs, outright sabotage of factories, and in other countless small but cumulatively important ways over which the government can exercise little punitive control. As the fate of the government of Deng Xiaoping and Li Peng shifts from politics to economics, where no amount of repression will be able to stem the tide of collapse, it becomes less and less difficult to imagine how another leader with a different notion of salvation for China might ascend to the top of the Gate of Heavenly Peace and proclaim that the "broad masses" had once again "stood up" to found a new government.

Davy (VU)

THE GATE AND

THE SQUARE

The night of June 3 I gave my last speech at Beijing Normal University. Before more than 20,000 people I said: "Today, every Chinese faces a choice. Chinese history is about to turn a new page. Tiananmen Square is ours, the people's, and we will not allow butchers to tread on it. We will defend Tiananmen Square, defend the students in the square, and defend the future of China." We asked them to sing the "Anti-Japanese March"—our national anthem since 1949—which includes the lines, "The Chinese people have reached their most critical moment. Everyone must join the final rally. Arise! Arise!"

—Wuer Kaixi, 1989 student leader from Beijing Normal University

Tiananmen Square, where so many of the impassioned events of the spring of 1989 unfolded, is the most emotionally and historically charged urban space in China. Tiananmen Gate itself—The Gate of Heavenly Peace—is at once the entryway into the inner vastness of the Forbidden City as well as the exit from that imperial and bureaucratic world into the zones of public space and revolutionary memory. In the ninety-acre square in front of it stand the massive monument to China's revolutionary martyrs, also known as the Monument to the People's Heroes, and the mausoleum containing the embalmed remains of Mao Zedong. On either side of the square are the huge buildings that house the National People's Congress and the museums of revolutionary history. To the east and west run some of Beijing's busiest boulevards, with their government offices and big hotels; off these arteries lies a maze of narrow streets and alleys filled with the hubbub of stores and small restaurants. To create a rough parallel in modern American life, one might think of the Mall in Washington, D.C., boardered by the White House on one side, the Lincoln Memorial on another, and running approximately from the Washington Monument to the Capitol.

The original version of the Tiananmen was built in the 1420s when an emperor of the ruling Ming Dynasty, which controlled China from 1368 to 1644, moved the capital from Nanjing on the Yangzi River to Beijing. The city, built on the orders of the Ming emperors, was in two segments. The inner segment, housing the emperor himself and his many consorts and children and the main audience halls—what is now called the Forbidden City—was protected by a wall twenty-two feet high, thirty feet thick, and two and a quarter miles long. This inner palace complex was itself completely surrounded by a second palace and temple complex—the Imperial City—where the emperor's more distant relatives

were housed and the offices of many administrative bureaus were located.

The Imperial City covered almost two square miles and was enclosed within a wall eighteen feet high and describing a six-and-a-half mile circumference. Outside the Imperial City were the residences of the bureaucrats and their families, and then the shopkeepers and citizens of Beijing. This whole area of close to twelve square miles was protected in turn by a third set of walls; these were sixty-two feet thick at the base and forty-one feet high. It was a colossal concept beautifully executed.

The Tiananmen Gate itself, the central southern entrance to the Imperial City, was on a geometrically precise axis that led north between the main ancestral temples to the Wumen, or Meridian Gate, that guarded the Forbidden City, and south to the outer line of defense. According to the cosmological and geomantic descriptions offered to the Ming emperor by a Chinese scholar involved in the planning, the Imperial and Forbidden City structure was a macrocosm of the human body. The Forbidden City represented the viscera and intestines, and points on the outer defensive perimeter walls the heads, shoulders, hands, and feet. In this scheme the Tiananmen represented the protective tissue around the heart, and the avenue that led to the gate was the lungs.

Under the Ming emperors and their Qing successors (who ruled China from 1644 to 1912), Tiananmen played a significant role in the rituals of royal governance. Edicts issued by the emperor within his Forbidden City audience chambers were carried on elaborate trays, protected by yellow umbrellas, through the Meridian Gate and down the long avenue between the ancestral altars to the platform above the main arches of Tiananmen. There, as the officials of the relevant ministries knelt by the little stream that runs under the five marble bridges to the south of Tiananmen, a court official declaimed the edicts aloud. The edicts were then ceremoniously lowered to the waiting officials beneath for copying and distribution around the country.

Under the Ming and Qing rulers there was no open Tiananmen Square as there is today. Instead, the space was composed of an unusual T-shaped walled courtyard on each side of which were clustered the neatly aligned rows of offices assigned to various ministries, military bureaus, and other government agencies.

The symbolism of Tiananmen Gate and its role in central rule could be seen in many other elements: from the mythical animals decorating the roof, whose task was to protect the inner palaces from fire, to the great ornamental stone pillars that stand in front of and behind the gate, each

CHILDREN OF THE DRAGON

topped by a mythical animal in a swirl of clouds. These animals watched over the rulers' conduct—those to the north observing their deportment in the palace, those to the south observing how the rulers treated their people. In their early original form, according to chronicles, such pillars had been made of wood, and any Chinese who wished to could carve his criticisms of his ruler into the wood, and the ruler was duty-bound to read it.

Tiananmen and its front courtyard were thus initially symbolic, ritualistic, and bureaucratic spaces. They became a public space only at moments of grave national crisis. One such moment occurred in 1644, when Li Zicheng, a peasant rebel from Shaanxi Province, seized the city of Beijing. During the heavy fighting that ensued, Tiananmen was badly damaged, perhaps almost destroyed. The gateway that we see today, with its five archways and elaborate superstructure, is a reconstructed version that was completed in 1651.

The next important intruders into the Forbidden City were foreigners. British and French troops, who fought their way to Beijing in 1860 in order to force the Qing emperor to allow residence in Beijing to their diplomatic personnel, bivouacked near the gate and briefly considered burning the whole Forbidden City to the ground in retaliation for the murder of some of their negotiators by the Qing. Deciding to preserve the city, they marched to the northwest suburbs of Beijing instead and burned the emperor's exquisite summer palace complex.

Once the Qing emperor capitulated to their demands, the foreign powers established a "legation quarter" for their diplomatic staffs just to the southeast of Tiananmen, on an area of land stretching one mile from east to west, and about half a mile north to south. When the antiforeign and anti-Christian society known as the Boxers rebelled in 1900, it was in this area of the city that they besieged the foreigners for a tense seven weeks of heavy fighting; the siege, actively encouraged by the Qing's redoubtable Empress Dowager Cixi, was only lifted when a joint expeditionary force of foreign troops fought its way through to Beijing from the coast at Tianjin. There was heavy damage to the office complex south of Tiananmen, and several of the ministries were burned down. The Qing court fled the city for the northwest as the allied armies entered the city. This time the Western troops forced their way through Tiananmen into the Forbidden City, which was used for a time as the headquarters of the Western armies. The space in front of Tiananmen became an assembly area for foreign troops and their horses.

The Qing dynasty collapsed in 1912, fatally weakened by a series of provincial rebellions, and China became a republic, albeit a weak and troubled one. Sun Yat-sen, who had been fighting the Qing since the late 1890s in the hopes of establishing a constitutional republic, was named the provisional president in January 1912. He tried to establish Nanjing as China's new capital, as it had been in the early Ming, but he was outmaneuvered by the tough and politically astute former Qing general Yuan Shikai, who insisted that Beijing—where the bulk of troops loyal to Yuan were stationed—remain the capital. Yuan was so much more powerful militarily, that Sun agreed (Continued on page 22)

Seventy years before the Tiananmen Square massacre, students petitioned the government for freedom of speech and the right to free assembly after protesting the terms of the Versailles Treaty. With the help of workers and merchants, the students succeeded in effecting a change of government, and China did not sign. This contemporary account, "When Students Overthrew a Government," was written by Sidney D. Gamble, an American sociologist.

Early in the forenoon of June 3 students' lecture bands were on the streets of the capital in force and with determination. Delegations of ten went together, carrying the banners of their schools and signs bearing numbered designations of their teams. Each group had assigned to it a certain district of the city. In this district it took its stand at a prominent point, where its members proceeded to explain to all who would listen the details of the Shantung question and the imperative need of buying only Chinese goods instead of Japanese goods.

By afternoon high officials of the government had taken matters into their own hands, called out the military forces and ordered the arrest of the lecturers by military, gendarmes, and police. But the sympathy of the police for the students was so great that they made no real effort to arrest them until the soldiers appeared on the scene. Then the students were called on to give themselves up, which they did without disturbance.

As the regular jails of the city would not hold the large number of students pouring in, the police took over a detention camp. Soon from all over the city came groups of soldiers, gendarmes, and policemen bringing in students. By evening there were nearly three hundred lecturers confined in the university buildings, where they

the police took over the science department of the university, putting a sign over the door, "Second Peking Students' Prison." That night the police had almost 900 students under their care, and more were expected. The student organization was ready to send out 500 every day until all the students in Peking were arrested—and then there would be students from outside cities to carry on the work. By Thursday morning, June 5, the police saw they had a hopeless task and issued orders to stop the arrests. That evening the government surrendered and withdrew the guards from the student prison. That did not mean, however, that the students would leave.

Settling down to the task of waiting until the government should meet their demands and make it possible for them to leave the prison with their "face" restored, the students organized themselves into committees, each to be responsible for some part of the life of the community. The group that was to take care of the policing of the camp put a guard at the gate. No students were allowed to leave

had to make the best of a night without food or bedding, some of them pretty badly bruised by the handling the military had given them.

The next day the excitement was greater than ever. Five hundred students went out to lecture, with the definite intention of being arrested. Most of them carried their blankets and little packages of food.

Every few minutes a group of soldiers, gendarmes, and police would come through the big gateway in the red wall of the imperial city, turn north along the moat, leading a group of students across the bridge. And all the time their quarry was cheering and shouting. The last cheer they gave as they went over the bridge was "Long live the republic!" The answering cheer from those who were already inside was "Long live the students!"

Before the third day was over the law college was nearly full, so and no visitors were allowed inside the grounds except on legitimate business. All those entering were required to give their names, addresses, and business before they were given a passport, and while they were inside the walls they were accompanied by a specially appointed student officer, who had to report to the head student official and secure from him a second passport before the visitors could leave.

Another committee was responsible for working out the policy that the student body should follow in its relations with the government. As a result of this committee's work four demands, approved by the student committee, were sent to the government:

1. That the students should be given the right to free speech and the privilege of lecturing wherever they desired.
2. That the government should apologize to the students for having wrongfully arrested them.
3. That a police guard should be given the students as they left

Student demonstration, November 29, 1919.   *Sydney Gamble*

their prison and marched throughout the city.

4. That the students should have the right of making a demonstration throughout the city.

Three of these demands the government granted. It permitted the students their demonstration and their lectures; also an official was sent to address the students, and although his words were half-hearted, they were such that the students could consider them an apology; but the police escort was refused. Monday morning their lecture bands were read all over the city making the most of the freedom they had won.

The culmination of the students' triumph began June 8, when three ministers resigned. No sooner had these men left than the whole cabinet resigned, and the president sent his letter of resignation to parliament. The students, with the help of the merchants, had forced a change of government.

—From *The Continent,* January 29, 1920

(Continued from page 19) to have Yuan named provisional president in his place. Realizing the symbolic importance of Tiananmen as the focus of central power, Yuan ordered his troops massed in front of the gate and received them there in huge parades at the time of his inauguration.

The boy emperor Puyi—who had been forced to abdicate in early 1912—was allowed to remain with his family, retainers, and eunuchs in the northern part of the Forbidden City, along with most of the Qing palace treasures. The area between Tiananmen and the first courtyards north of the Meridian Gate (Wumen) were, however, nationalized and became the seat for some government offices and museums.

The Tiananmen courtyard was featured in two other major public events at this time. One was the funeral of Yuan Shikai, who died in 1916 after being humiliatingly rebuffed by provincial generals and politicians when he tried to proclaim himself emperor instead of president. Despite this fiasco, the funeral was a grand event, a true public spectacle. The other was more bizarre, the attempt by a Manchu-loyalist general named Zhang Xun to restore the abdicated boy emperor Puyi—then aged eleven—to the throne. For a few days Zhang's troops occupied the square and the Forbidden City, and the old imperial dragon flags flew once again. But after Zhang's defeat by armies loyal to the republic, new restrictions were placed on Puyi, and he was expelled from the palace in 1924. The whole Forbidden City area was nationalized and turned into tourist sites, staff offices, and museums, and the courtyard became a true public square.

During this period the city of Beijing underwent great changes that altered the symbolic importance of Tiananmen Square. Slowly, the square became a natural forum for rallies and debates over national policy, in part because the area was becoming a political and educational hub. Not only was the new Department of Justice here on the west side, and the new Parliament just farther west beyond the department, but the area was also the site of a host of universities and colleges, now becoming, with the demise of the old imperial system, the focus for the career hopes of young, ambitious Chinese men and women. The three main campus units of Beijing University—those for literature, science, and law—were all just to the east of the Forbidden City, an easy walk to the square. More than a dozen other colleges were clustered near the square, mainly to its west, including several schools and colleges for women and the prestigious Qinghua College, where many students prepared their English language skills before going off to the United States to study.

The rally and demonstration that had the greatest impact on this whole period of Chinese history was that of May 4, 1919. On that day 3,000 student representatives from thirteen area universities and colleges gathered in the square to protest the disastrous terms of the Versailles Treaty, in which the victorious allies granted several former German concessions in China to the Japanese, who had signed secret

The Museum of the Chinese Revolution, 1965.
René Burri (Magnum)

agreements with the Allies before joining their side in the war. The Chinese were outraged. They had also been on the side of the Allies and had sent more than 100,000 laborers to work the trenches, docks, and supply lines of the British and French forces. Now they were crudely rebuffed.

The protests begun on May 4 inaugurated a new phase of national consciousness in China and firmly fixed in the nation's mind the idea of the square as a political focal point. Small scale when compared to the 1989 demonstrations, May 4 nevertheless roused the nation's conscience, and the term "May 4 Movement" was adopted to describe the entire event as Chinese scholars, scientists, writers, and artists struggled to explore new ways of strengthening China and incorporating the twin forces of science and democracy into the life of their society and government. Linked in its turn to a study of the plight of China's workers and peasants, and

October 1, 1949. Mao declares the founding of the People's Republic of China. *(Magnum/Xinhua)*

to the theoretical and organizational arguments of Marxism-Leninism, the May 4 Movement had a direct bearing and influence on the growth of the Chinese Communist Party (CCP), which convened its first congress in 1921.

If 1919 marked Tiananmen Square's inauguration as a fully public and antigovernmental space, the 1920s saw its true baptism of fire. These were terrible years in the history of the Chinese republic. The Beijing government was corrupt, ineffective, and the pawn of a succession of militarists or warlords. Other warlords controlled sections of China, sometimes whole provinces, sometimes scattered cities or stretches of countryside. Foreign economic and political exploration of China continued unabated; Japanese assaults on China's territory grew ever more determined. Antiforeign outrage reached a new peak on May 30, 1925, in Shanghai, after British police killed forty or more Chinese demonstrators at a major rally. The inhabitants of Beijing responded with a vast sympathy rally of their own, and Tiananmen Square was the natural, chosen location to hold it.

Celebrating three years of statehood,
October 1, 1952.
(Sovfoto)

Henri Cartier-Bresson (Magnum)

Mao and Liu Shaoqi *(second from left)* at a rally protesting the American presence in Vietnam, 1965.

Ta Hsiuhsien (Sovfoto)

A public rostrum in front of Tiananmen Gate was covered with the slogans of the day: "Abolish Unequal Treaties," "Boycott English and Japanese Products," "Down with the Great Powers." Paper banners with political slogans fluttered from the trees—the square was more like a public park than the sterile space it is today—and other slogans were scrawled in black ink or charcoal on the walls of adjacent buildings. Student pickets kept order, and police and army troops kept their distance.

But as demonstration followed demonstration that fall and winter, the patience of local authorities faded. At last, on March 18, 1926, the long-anticipated violence on the part of the authorities erupted. A fresh crowd of 6,000 or more, drawn mainly from students and labor groups, met at Tiananmen to protest the warlord government's spineless acceptance of new Japanese demands. After emotional speeches, the crowd moved off toward the cabinet office of the Beijing-based government. Regular troops opened fire on the crowd without attempting to disperse them first—at least fifty were killed, and 200 or more wounded. It was the first such massacre in China's history, but it would not be the last. "Lies written in ink can never disguise facts written in blood," exclaimed China's best-known writer, Lu Xun, several of

whose own students were among the dead. "Blood debts must be repaid in kind, the longer the delay, the greater the interest."

The importance of Tiananmen Square as a public space decreased for a while after 1928, for Chiang Kai-shek's troops and their allies nominally united the country that year and declared Nanjing the nation's capital. Beijing, now renamed Beiping, lost its central role, and as government bureaus relocated to Nanjing, student protests in Tiananmen lost much of their former significance, though Sun Yatsen's portrait now hung over the central arch of Tiananmen Gate. An exception was the demonstration held on December 9, 1935, when students and citizens met in the square to protest Chiang Kai-shek's continued appeasement of Japan. The city police, who had tried to prevent the demonstration by blocking the gates into the square, used violence against the students, turning the fire hoses on them in the near-freezing weather. Though the impact was not as great as that of May 4, 1919, or March 18, 1926, the "December Niners," as they were swiftly dubbed by the public, did become a potent symbol to the country as a whole of anti-Japanese resistance.

Beijing lost many of its students after 1938, when Japan's full-scale invasion of China led to the retreat of

1966. A half-million Red Guards
at a rally for Mao.
(Sovfoto)

Chiang's armies deep inland to the west. The Communists, for their part, now led by Mao Zedong, made their own base in Shaanxi and attracted many radical students. The Japanese, meanwhile, decorated Tiananmen Gate and Square with colored lights and used it to hold various pro-Japanese rallies and to review the troops of their puppet allies. In 1945, with Japan's defeat and the return of the students from the southwest, the square again became the focus for rallies. This time they were lead by radicals and were against Chiang Kai-shek, for the Communists and Nationalists were now locked in a civil war for control of the country.

Mao Zedong and the Communist party re-created Tiananmen as both a public and an official space. As the Communist victory became a reality in late September 1949, Mao convened a series of meetings in Beiping to consider the country's future course, though there was never any doubt that he intended the country to follow the orders of the Communists themselves. To underline this point, the front of Tiananmen was bedecked with two giant photographs, facing out across the square. One was of Mao Zedong himself; the other was of Mao's leading general, Zhu De, the builder of the Red Army and its finest leader during the long years of guerrilla fighting. On September 30, Mao led the delegates out into the walled square. At a spot 875 yards south of Tiananmen Gate, they broke ground for a Monument to the People's Heroes that was to arise on the central axis between the palace gates. And on October 1, 1949, before cheering crowds, Mao mounted the platform above the Tiananmen Gate in the city now renamed Beijing and declared the founding of the new People's Republic of China.

Tiananmen now became the Communist government's preeminent public space. As the parades grew more grandiose, the square began to take on its present form. In 1958 the remaining walls were torn down, along with the buildings sheltered behind them, and the square was extended to a space of over forty hectares (one hectare equals 2.47 acres), a size that would allow one million people at a time to assemble there. Two huge buildings were constructed, on opposite sides of the square, to house the National People's Congress and the museums of the revolution. That same year, the ornate monolith to the martyrs of China's century

A million people gather upon the death of Zhou Enlai, 1976. *Luo Xiaoyun*

Mao's memorial service, Changan Avenue, 1976. *Hiroshi Nakanishi (Mainichi Shimbun)*

or more of revolutionary struggle, the new square's center-piece, was completed. For May Day rallies and October 1 anniversaries, Mao and all the central Communist leadership would stand upon the Tiananmen Gate, gazing out over their people in the square, while another 10,000 or so officials and invited guests crowded the reviewing stands just below them, along the wall of the former Imperial City.

In 1966, as Mao launched the cataclysmic Cultural Revolution, first hundreds of thousands, and then as many as a million of the so-called Red Guards marched in serried ranks before him, cheering and waving the red book of his selected speeches, as they dedicated themselves to lives of "revolutionary purity" in his name. Fired up by such rallies, Red Guards fanned out across the city, and thence across the country, to root out any of those in power who had ties to the old order or could be accused of "bureaucratism" or lack

Mao's memorial service.
Hiroshi Nakanishi (Mainichi Shimbun)

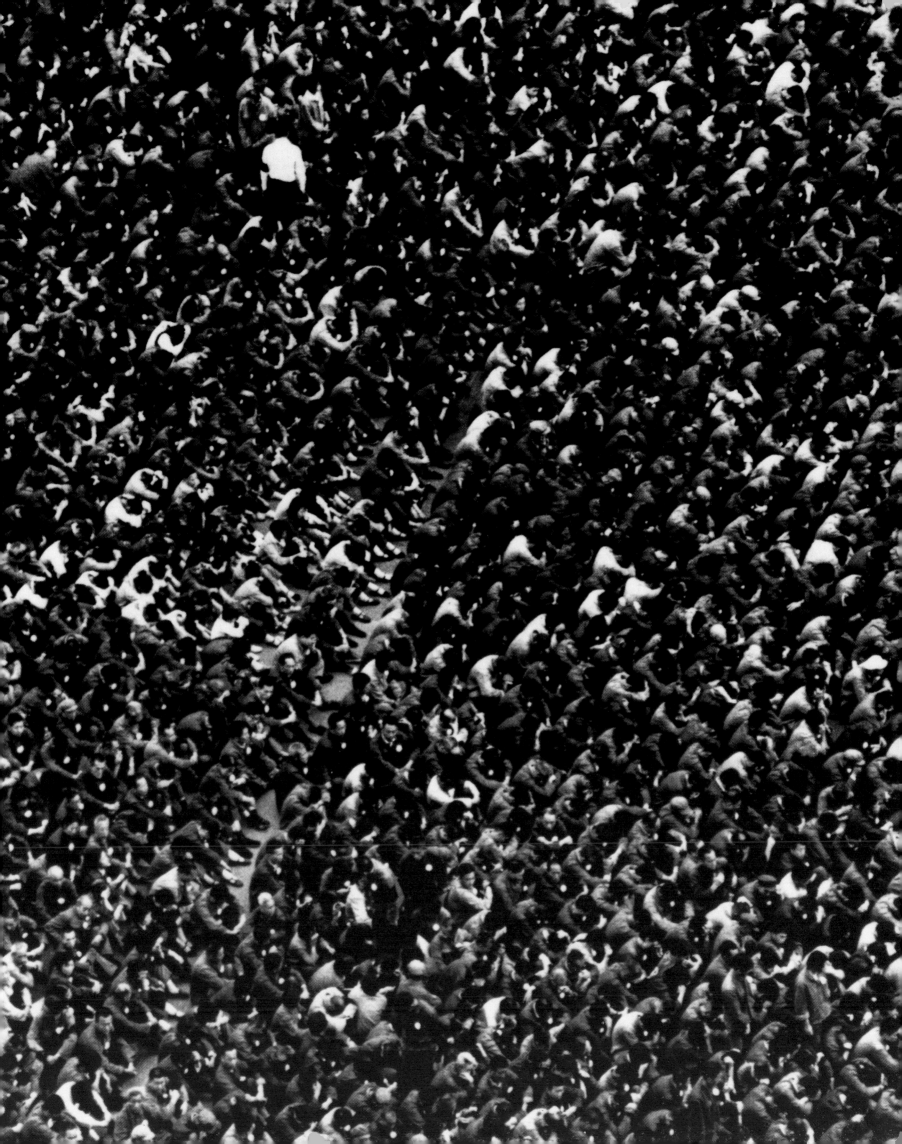

of revolutionary zeal. Among those seized, dismissed, mal-treated, and publicly humiliated was Deng Xiaoping. One can guess that in 1989, the din of the rallies of the Cultural Revolution reverberated in Deng's ears above the calls for democracy and the chanting of slogans and pop music from the student's loudspeakers in the square.

The colleges and universities were almost all moved to the outskirts of Beijing by the government in the first years of the People's Republic. The alleged reasons for these moves were practical ones, based on the need for space and facilities. But if the government wanted to preserve the square for itself, it certainly made the task easier by placing Beida, Qinghua, and the other prestigious schools in the far northwest of the city, a four-hour walk or one-hour-plus bike ride from the square, with no subway links and an erratic bus service, which required several changes.

1979. The Democracy Wall. *Liu Heung Shing (Contact Press Images)*

Tourists on the square. *Liu Heung Shing (Contact Press Images)*

High school students.
Liu Heung Shing
(Contact Press Images)

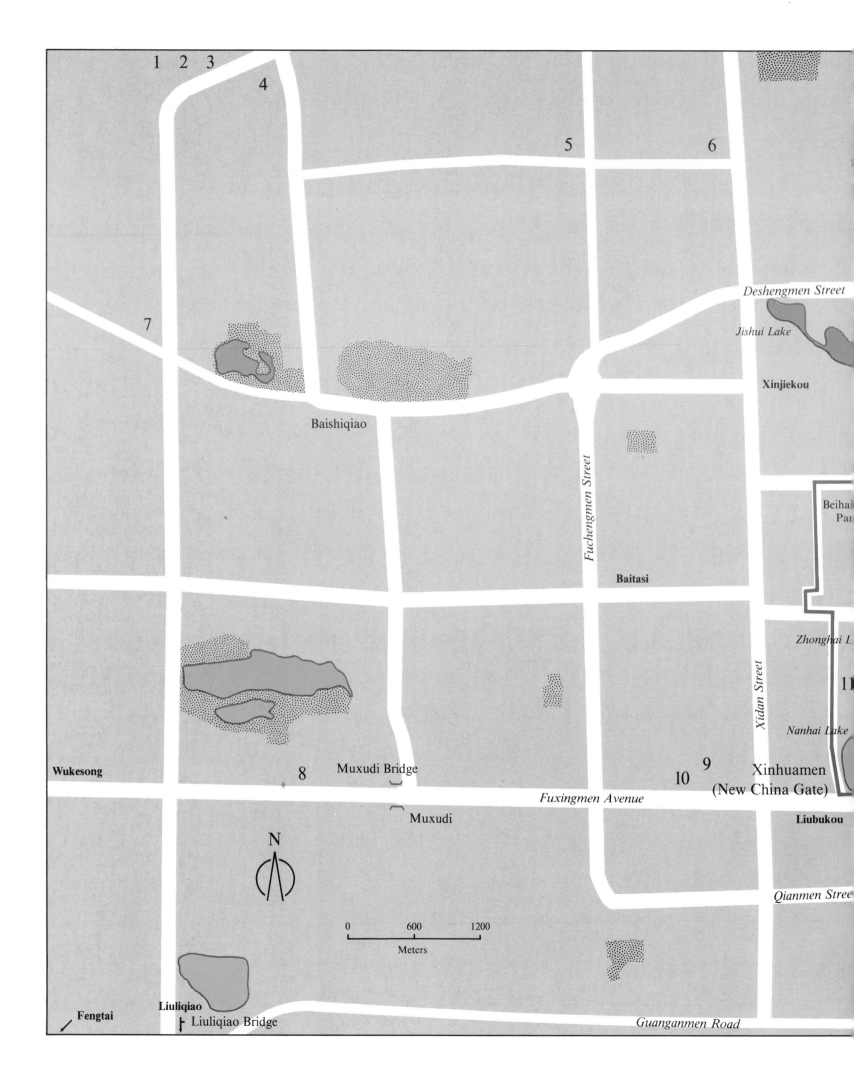

1 2 3

4

5 6

7

Deshengmen Street

Jishui Lake

Xinjiekou

Baishiqiao

Fuchengmen Street

Beiha
Par

Baitasi

Zhonghai L

Xidan Street

1

Nanhai Lake

Wukesong

8 Muxudi Bridge

10 9

Xinhuamen
(New China Gate)

Muxudi

Liubukou

N

Fuxingmen Avenue

Qianmen Stree

0   600   1200

Meters

Liuliqiao

Fengtai   ├ Liuliqiao Bridge

Guanganmen Road

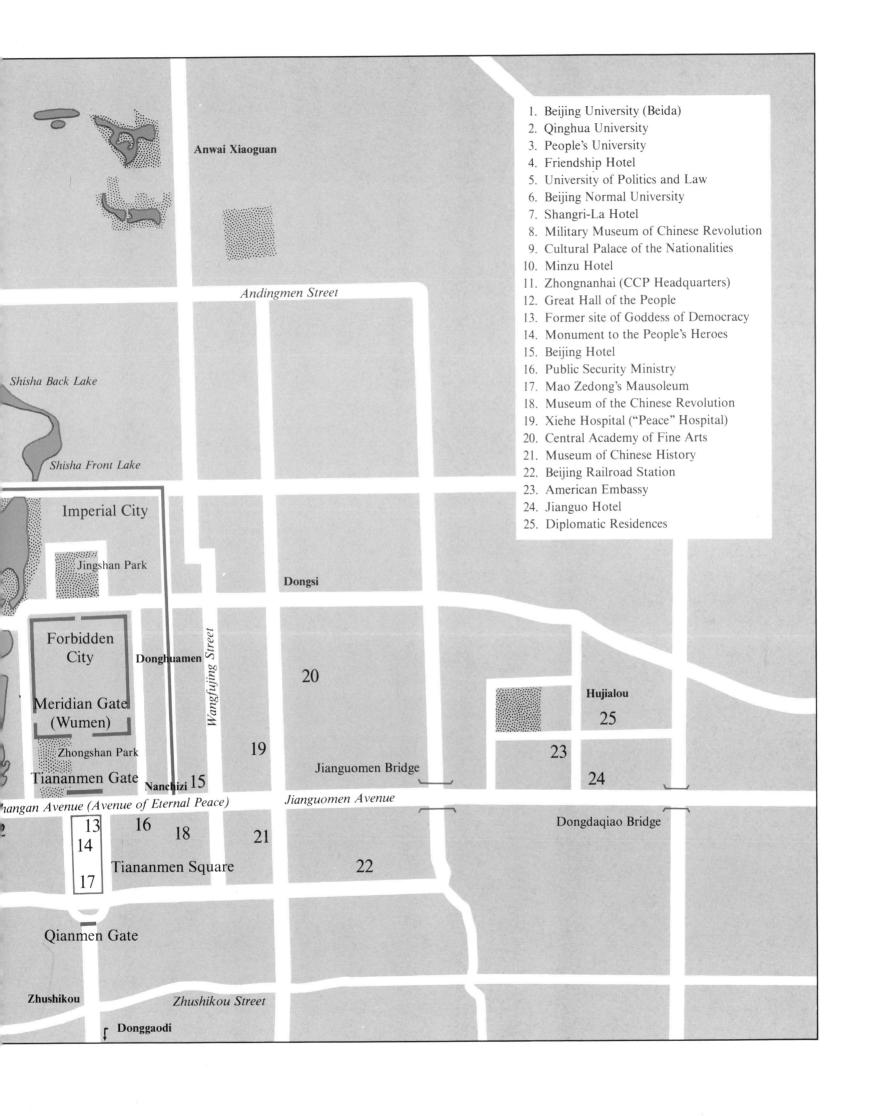

1. Beijing University (Beida)
2. Qinghua University
3. People's University
4. Friendship Hotel
5. University of Politics and Law
6. Beijing Normal University
7. Shangri-La Hotel
8. Military Museum of Chinese Revolution
9. Cultural Palace of the Nationalities
10. Minzu Hotel
11. Zhongnanhai (CCP Headquarters)
12. Great Hall of the People
13. Former site of Goddess of Democracy
14. Monument to the People's Heroes
15. Beijing Hotel
16. Public Security Ministry
17. Mao Zedong's Mausoleum
18. Museum of the Chinese Revolution
19. Xiehe Hospital ("Peace" Hospital)
20. Central Academy of Fine Arts
21. Museum of Chinese History
22. Beijing Railroad Station
23. American Embassy
24. Jianguo Hotel
25. Diplomatic Residences

Anwai Xiaoguan

Andingmen Street

Shisha Back Lake

Shisha Front Lake

Imperial City

Jingshan Park

Dongsi

Forbidden City

Donghuamen

Wangfujing Street

Meridian Gate (Wumen)

Zhongshan Park

Tiananmen Gate

Nanchizi 15

13
14
17

16

18

21

Tiananmen Square

22

20

Hujialou

25

23

24

Jianguomen Bridge

Jianguomen Avenue

Dongdaqiao Bridge

Changan Avenue (Avenue of Eternal Peace)

19

Qianmen Gate

Zhushikou

Zhushikou Street

Donggaodi

LET THE WHOLE

WORLD KNOW!

WHO'S WHO

Bao Tong: Former personal secretary and senior advisor to Zhao Ziyang as well as former secretary of Politburo and member of Party Central Committee. In 1987, he was named head of the Research Center for Political Structural Reform. May have been arrested prior to June 3.

Bao Zunxin: Magazine editor and associate research fellow at the Institute of Chinese History under the Chinese Academy of Social Sciences (CASS). He is believed to have been arrested.

Bo Yibo: Vice-chairman of Party Central Advisory Commission; former Politburo member and vice-premier.

Cai Chongguo: Doctoral candidate at Wuhan University. He now lives in Paris.

Cao Xinyuan: A sculptor from Beijing; she is now a graduate student in art history at the University of California, Berkeley.

Cha J.: Lecturer at People's University. She is now a visiting scholar at Columbia University.

Chai Ling: Former graduate student in psychology at Beijing Normal University, student leader, and commander in chief of Tiananmen demonstrators. She is presently living in France.

Chen Mingyuan: Former professor at Beijing Foreign Language Institute, where he taught Chinese to foreigners. He is believed to have been arrested shortly after the crackdown.

Chen Yizi: Leading advisor to Zhao Ziyang. He was the head of the Institute of Economic Reform. He is now living in the United States.

Cunningham, Phillip: Graduate student in Chinese history at the University of Michigan.

Dai Qing: Reporter for *Guangming Ribao (Enlightenment Daily)*. China's leading female journalist and the adopted daughter of Ye Jianying, former marshal of the People's Liberation Army (PLA). She was arrested after the June crackdown.

Deng Xiaoping: Former chairman of the Party Central Military Commission. Although he now lacks any official titles and has officially resigned from his positions in the Party, he still wields tremendous influence over Chinese politics and was considered by many as China's supreme leader during the 1989 demonstrations and ensuing crackdown.

Fang Lizhi: Astrophysicist, dissident, and former vice-president of the University of Science and Technology in Hefei, Anhui Province. He was expelled from the Chinese Communist Party (CCP) in 1987 following the student demonstrations. In early June, he and his wife, Li Shuxian, were granted refuge at the U.S. embassy in Beijing.

Fei Xiaotong: Leading sociologist and chairman of the China Democratic League. He is still in China.

Feng Congde: Husband of Chai Ling; former postgraduate student at Beijing Remote Sensing Institute. He is presently living in France.

Gao Huan (pseudonym): Student from Qinghua University.

Gao Xin: Former editor of the Beijing Normal University *Gazette*. One of the June 2 hunger-strikers. He is believed to have been imprisoned.

Ge Yang: Former editor in chief of *New Observer* magazine, which was banned by Chinese authorities for supporting the students. She is now in the United States.

Gu Benxi: Lieutenant colonel in the PLA. He was one of the commanders of the operation to clear Tiananmen Square in the early hours of June 4, 1989.

Hou Dejian: A Taiwanese singer who defected to the mainland in 1983. One of the June 2 hunger-strikers. He is still in China.

Hou Tianming: Lawyer from Beijing. He left Beijing after the massacre and now lives in Paris.

Hu Ping: Leader of 1980 Chinese student movement. Now in the United States, he is the head of the Chinese Alliance for Democracy.

Hu Qili: Former Politburo member and propaganda chief. He was dismissed from his posts in June 1989.

Hu Yaobang: General secretary of the CCP from 1981 to 1987. Forced to resign in the wake of student demonstrations in early 1987; his death, on April 15, 1989, was the immediate catalyst for the 1989 pro-democracy movement.

Huang Yan (pseudonym): Student at Beijing Normal University.

Ji Xinguo: Along with Lieutenant Colonel Gu Benxi, he led the operation to clear Tiananmen Square in the early morning of June 4; he negotiated with Hou Dejian.

Jiang Zemin: Former Party secretary of Shanghai. In 1989, Jiang succeeded Zhao Ziyang as general secretary of the CCP.

Lao Gui ("Old Devil"): A leading novelist and author of the best-selling novel *Bloody Sunset*. He now lives in the United States.

Li Honglin: Reformer; research fellow at the Fujian Academy of Social Sciences, in Fujian Province. He is believed to have been arrested on June 6, 1989.

Li Lu: Student leader from Nanjing University. He is now in the United States.

Li Zehou: A present-day Chinese philosopher and writer.

Link, Perry: Leading China scholar. He is a professor of Chinese literature at Princeton University.

Liu Binyan: Preeminent Chinese journalist and an outspoken critic of Party corruption. Purged from the Communist party and sentenced to labor reform in 1957, he was "rehabilitated" in 1979 but expelled again in the 1987 campaign against bourgeois liberalism. He was a Nieman Fellow at Harvard University and is currently a distinguished writer in residence at Trinity College in Hartford, Connecticut.

Liu Tang (pseudonym): A Beijing student.

Liu Xiaobo: Professor in Chinese at Beijing Normal University. He was arrested after staging a hunger strike on June 2.

Lu Dingyi: Former propaganda minister of the CCP.

Ma Shaofang: Student at Beijing Film Academy and associate of Wuer Kaixi. He was reported to have turned himself in to authorities in Guangzhou on June 17, 1989.

Munro, Robin: Senior research associate for Asia Watch in New York City. He translated Chen Erjin's *China: Crossroads Socialism,* a key text of the Democracy Wall movement.

Peng Ling (pseudonym): A Beijing student now living in New York City.

Qiao Shi: Member of the Standing Committee of the Politburo in charge of legal and security matters. Among his other duties, he is the head of the Chinese secret police.

Ruan Ming: Former department head of Central Party Academy and long-time personal friend of Hu Yaobang. He is currently a visiting scholar at Columbia University.

Shen Tong: Student leader from Beijing University. He is now studying at Brandeis University.

Shi Renquan: Officer in the PLA. He was among the martial law troops that occupied Beijing.

Su Wei: Literary critic; served as liaison between intellectuals and students in Tiananmen Square. He is now at the University of Chicago.

Su Xiaokang: Journalist and co-author of the television series "River Elegy," which has been criticized and banned by the CCP. He escaped to Paris.

Tao Ye: Member of the Autonomous Workers' Federation.

Wan Li: Chairman of the National People's Congress. He has been a member of the Politburo since 1982.

Wan Runnan: Former chairman of Stone Computer Corporation, a computer manufacturer and China's largest private enterprise. He is now the general secretary of the Federation for a Democratic China.

Wang Chaohua: A student from the Chinese Academy of Social Sciences (CASS). Her whereabouts are unknown.

Wang Dan: Student leader from Beijing University. He was arrested following the June 4 massacre.

Wei Jingsheng: Activist during the 1978–79 Democracy Wall movement. He was sentenced to fifteen years in jail as a result.

Wen Yuankai: Chairman of the chemistry department at the University of Science and Technology in Hebei Province.

Wuer Kaixi (Uerkesh Daolet): 1989 student leader from Beijing Normal University and a founding member of Federation for a Democratic China in Paris. He is a member of the Uighur minority, originally from Xinjiang Province, in western China. Wuer Kaixi is now a student at Harvard University.

Yan Jiaqi: Leading advocate of economic and political reform; former director of the Political Studies Institute at CASS and former advisor to top officials including Zhao Ziyang. He is currently in exile in Paris, where he helped launch the Federation for a Democratic China.

Yan Mingfu: Minister of the United Front and vice-chairman of the National People's Consultative Committee. He was elected secretary of the Party Secretariat in 1987.

Yang Jianli: Presently a graduate student in mathematics at the University of California, Berkeley.

Yang Shangkun: President of the People's Republic of China and vice-chairman of the Central Military Commission. His influence with the army is believed to have contributed to the military crackdown in June.

Yu Shuo: Professor of philosophy at People's University. She is now living in Paris.

Yuan Mu: Former journalist. Since 1988 he has been the spokesman for the State Council, which is the highest organ of state administration and the executive body of the National People's Congress.

Yuan Zhiming: Former graduate student in philosophy at People's University and co-author of "River Elegy." He now lives in Paris.

Zhang Boli: Student at Beijing University and one of the founding members of the Provisional Student Union. His whereabouts are unknown.

Zhang Langlang: A former Red Guard who was imprisoned for ten years for opposing Jiang Qing, Mao's widow. He now lives in the United States.

Zhao Ziyang: General secretary of the Communist party from 1987 to 1989. Officially removed from power following the June 4 crackdown; his current status is unknown.

Zheng Yi: A writer best known for his novel *Old Well,* which was made into a very successful and popular movie. He is believed to have been arrested.

Zhou Duo: An economist with the Stone Corporation and a June 2 hunger-striker. He was arrested on July 10.

Zhou Enlai: Premier of China from 1949 until his death in 1976.

THE DEATH OF

HU YAOBANG

On April 15, I attended a farewell party for departing U.S. Ambassador Winston Lord and his wife, Bette Bao Lord. I rarely go to these foreign gatherings, and I felt a little bit inferior because I was a dirty old devil*—a horse-cart driver from Inner Mongolia—but now I was a guest of the American ambassador.

Bette Lord, dressed all in red and looking like flames, greeted everyone with warmth and politeness. As I tapped my feet to the music, Zhang Langlang came over and quietly asked, "Did you hear that Hu Yaobang passed away this morning?"

I couldn't believe my ears. "What happened to Hu Yaobang?"

"He died this morning."

The news was too sudden. I wasn't prepared for it, and I immediately lost my enthusiasm for the party.

In 1986, I had sent copies of my first novel, *Bloody Sunset,*† to the two leaders I respected most—both of whom were out of favor at the time—Hu Yaobang and Lu Dingyi. I thought they had the guts to tell the truth, to stick to their principles, and to free themselves from Maoist ideology. On the inside cover of the copy I sent to Hu I wrote:

Dear Comrade Hu Yaobang:
In 1967, when you were being publicly denounced

---

* Lao Gui, the author's pseudonym, means "old devil."
† *Bloody Sunset,* one of the new breed of journalistic novels, is a commentary on disillusioned Red Guards who were sent to the countryside during the Cultural Revolution.

A gathering near the Monument to the People's Heroes.
Patrick Zachmann (Magnum)

Students pay tribute to Hu Yaobang.

at the Beijing Exhibition Hall, I was one of the two Red Guards* who twisted your arms during your criticism.† But today, twenty-one years later, I love and respect you. And people throughout the country understand you and will never forget you.

Hu had brought only a tiny bit of democracy and freedom to the Chinese people. In turn, he lost his position as general secretary.

Personally, I'm very grateful to Hu Yaobang for creating a relaxed atmosphere unprecedented for Chinese artists and writers. It enabled the Workers' Publishing House to publish *Bloody Sunset*.

Hu made more contributions to China than Zhou Enlai, and he had much more integrity than Zhou. But now he is gone. I feel so sad, even sadder than when my father died.

If Deng Xiaoping had not persecuted him, he would not have died so young. Damn it!

On my way out of the party I bumped into Dai Qing. Lowering my voice I told her, "Hu Yaobang is gone."

"Yes, I know," she replied, her eyes understanding.

"Do you think something like April 5 will happen again?" I asked.‡

"That depends on how the authorities handle his funeral. If they accord him the high honors he deserves, people won't make a fuss. Otherwise, it could be another April 5," she replied. "I know that some students are prepared to cause a scene. Their eyes are wide open, waiting to see what will happen."

On Sunday, April 16, I went to Tiananmen Square. Someone had already put a large wreath there. The monument was surrounded by a metal chain. Nobody was sup-

---

* The Red Guards were Chinese youths who "defended the Communist party" against its "enemies" during the Cultural Revolution.
† When someone was publicly denounced during the Cultural Revolution, he was placed on a stage while two people stood behind him and twisted his arms behind his back until he was forced to bend over as others read criticisms of him.

‡ On April 5, 1976, over one million people from Beijing spontaneously filled Tiananmen Square to mourn the death of Premier Zhou Enlai and express anger against the Gang of Four, the ultra-leftist group, headed by Mao's wife, Jiang Qing, that controlled the government. The incident resulted in a bloody crackdown on the night of April 5, which is now known as the April 5, or Tiananmen Incident.

Rally, in the days after Hu's death.
Abbas (Magnum)

Hu . . . was the only one in the Communist party who had any democratic ideas . . . he had genuine concern for the students and the plight of the people.

posed to get inside, and I didn't see any white paper flowers.* In front, I saw two policemen carrying pistols, their eyes on the crowd. I also saw some undercover police on the west side, speaking into walkie-talkies.

Monday, April 17, I returned to Tiananmen Square. Two more wreaths had been added to the monument, and the crowd around it was slightly larger. But there were too few wreaths there—they looked lonely, too small inside the huge square. I couldn't believe that the citizens of Beijing were so unfeeling. Hu Yaobang deserved more wreaths than Zhou Enlai; he was more deserving of the people's sympathy. Then, in the afternoon, I felt the atmosphere begin to change. People started pouring in from all directions. White paper flowers appeared on the hedges, and students from Beida put a huge banner around the base of the monument. It said: "The soul of the nation."

Tuesday, April 18, Tiananmen Square looked dramatically different from the past two days. A sea of people now surrounded the monument, and there were many wreaths in front of it. From time to time, lines of students arrived with wreaths. The armed policemen had disappeared.

At one o'clock in the afternoon I saw a huge crowd gathered around the west part of the square. Students from Qinghua, Beida,† and several other schools sat quietly in a circle under the blazing sun. They used newspaper to cover their heads and clothing to shade their faces from the harsh sunlight. People surrounded them, constantly donating money to buy soda and popsicles. Meanwhile, a student with a bullhorn repeatedly read their seven requests:

1. Reevaluate Hu Yaobang's achievements and mistakes.
2. Completely denounce the Anti–Spiritual Pollution and

---

* White paper flowers are traditionally used for mourning in China.

† Qinghua is China's leading scientific university. Beida is short for Beijing University.

When I first heard that Hu had died I couldn't believe my ears. . . . I was very happy, not that he had died, but that our opportunity had arrived.

Anti–Bourgeois Liberalization campaigns.*
3. Allow free press and freedom of speech.
4. Disclose the income of the leaders and their families.
5. Cancel the ten 1987 Beijing Municipal Regulations against demonstrations.
6. Increase spending for education and improve living standards for intellectuals.
7. Truthfully report the memorial activities.

Every time he finished reading one request, the crowd cheered and applauded thunderously. After I heard this, I felt as if each word came from the bottom of my heart. The students' words vented the anger I had kept pent up for the two long years since Hu had been forced to step down.

It surprised me that these most fashionable, most materialistic, most pragmatic university students were now sitting under the scorching sun almost the entire day. I took out ten yuan†—all I had on me—and bought them some drinks; then I went to sit under a pine tree, where I wrote them a note. I handed it to one of the Beijing University students I knew. It said, "Students, your seven requests represent the wishes of the people. I strongly support you. You got up first, openly crying out against the injustice done to Hu Yaobang. Well done! I salute you. The people will be grateful to you."

Several days later I heard from a friend at Beijing University that my letter had been posted on the campus.

—*Lao Gui, a popular novelist now living in exile*

China's leaders usually hide their real feelings and beliefs. Mao Zedong and Deng Xiaoping were able to keep people guessing. Hu Yaobang lacked that quality. He spoke his mind, so he made more visible mistakes than those who kept their true feelings concealed. When his judgments were wrong, he was willing to reverse himself. Some people believe Hu Yaobang was not meant to be a leader.

Politically, Hu was less astute than the old leaders such as Deng Xiaoping, but he was more intellectual than the second generation leaders like Zhao Ziyang. He read everything from Marx to Shakespeare and had great respect for knowledge and learned people. Unfortunately, Hu was not as skillful at political maneuvering. Although he represented a new style of politics that China needed, he was too weak to overcome old-style politics.

He felt that capitalism was not all evil, and that it should be looked at from a new perspective. He believed in the basic principles of Marxism, but at the same time he thought that Marx's predictions and the means of revolution he advocated were out of date.

The student movement paid tribute to Hu because he was the only one in the Communist party who had any democratic ideas. Some hoped that he would return to power. Now his death has left a vacuum in the Party. Although he was weak, he had genuine concern for the students and the plight of the people. His downfall was the direct outcome of a student movement, and it was natural that his memorial service touched off the last student movement. Hu's personal qualities accelerated the demonstrations into a large-scale movement involving people from all walks of life. In a sense, the pro-democracy movement was his epitaph.

—*Ruan Ming, former department head of the central party academy and long-time friend of Hu Yaobang*

We loved Hu Yaobang and we wanted to do something by way of remembrance. But that was not the main motivation of the movement. Its chief inspiration was, rather, the general craving for the democracy and openness that Hu Yaobang had promoted. As idealistic college students, we felt that China ought to be a genuine republic, and that the lingering "imperial system" must be finally abolished. The Republican Revolution of 1911 overthrew the last emperor. Nevertheless, even though the title has disappeared, an "emperor" has continued to exist. China is still run by the word of one man, and power remains unchecked; that, in turn, has given rise to profiteering, official corruption, and crushing bureaucracy.

—*Wuer Kaixi*

After the winter recess in 1989, I formed a student group at Beida. Learning from past experience, I chose the inconspicuous name of Scientific Seminar. Around the same time, Wang Dan formed his Democracy Salon, which absorbed most of the members of the Wednesday Forum.‡

In our group discussions we analyzed various aspects of China's political situation. We came to believe that Chinese intellectuals had, over the past few years, taken on the dimensions of a formal pressure group, or even an embryonic opposition party. We also decided that the coastal areas had developed so quickly, economically, that they had in effect

---

* The Anti–Spiritual Pollution campaign was a campaign mounted by the Chinese Communist Party (CCP) hard-liners to blame foreign influences for crime, corruption, pornography, and other social problems. The campaign lasted from October 1983 to February 1984. The Anti–Bourgeois Liberalization campaign was launched in early 1987 against intellectuals who advocated free speech and was prompted by widespread student protests.
† Ten yuan is approximately $3 U.S.

‡ The Wednesday Forum was a student group at Beida that met every Wednesday and invited prominent intellectuals such as Fang Lizhi, to give lectures.

Students in the provinces were more impatient than we were. A leader from Anhui wanted to start fasting on April 5, but we thought the time was not ripe.

detached themselves from the influence of ideology altogether.

Our analysis of the army was largely borne out by events. We saw that new recruits were mainly farmers who had benefited greatly from the reforms. Having a personal investment in the new economy, they were unlikely to be brainwashed easily or to obey orders blindly. Another part of the army was composed of young officers who had recently graduated from military schools. They were well educated and likely to be sympathetic to the democracy movement. At the very top were some 800 generals who were not very happy with Deng and Yang Shangkun. The only group that stood firmly against the student movement was the so-called Prince Clan, which included the sons of high officials. We concluded that the army would pose a threat to the 1989 pro-democracy movement but felt that if we did not go too far, they would not present a real danger.

In early 1989, many activists from the provinces came to Beijing—always visiting Beida first. We had some long and intense discussions with them, and made a detailed strategic plan. First, we looked for an opportunity to stage a major demonstration that would then be followed by a hunger strike. When the provincial schools began to move, we would consolidate the student organization and work out a theoretical outline. Finally, we would stage a huge demonstration in the fall. If we succeeded, we might even be able to bring Hu Yaobang back to power.

Students in the provinces were more impatient than we were. A leader from Anhui Province wanted to start fasting on April 5, but we thought the time was not yet ripe.

We all knew that a major political event would trigger

demonstrations, which would snowball quickly into a nationwide movement. Nineteen eighty-nine was a year of significant anniversaries: the tenth anniversary of the Beijing Democracy Wall, the fortieth anniversary of the founding of the PRC, the seventieth anniversary of the May 4 movement, and the bicentennial of the French Revolution. If we missed this year, however, we also knew that we might have to wait for a long time. All of us waited anxiously for an opportunity to come.

When I first heard that Hu had died, I couldn't believe my ears. I called several newspapers, but none of them could confirm the news. When I finally did confirm it, I was very happy, not that he had died, but that our opportunity had arrived.

—*Shen Tong, a student leader from Beijing University*

I gave my first speech on April 16, in Tiananmen Square. It was very short—lasting only a couple of minutes—about the problems of the Chinese educational system. I told my audience that during vacations I had traveled all over China to conduct research. I studied the situation of Chinese education quite extensively and found that the root of the problem lay in the socioeconomic system. Forty years after the establishment of the Communist government, education was still backward; because educational problems were rooted in the system, there could be no improvement in education until the system was changed.

We returned to the campus, and on April 17, I made another speech. Probably the only thing people will remember from that one was that I told everyone my name and

---

The 1989 pro-democracy movement was an inevitable product of the ten years of reform. The Cultural Revolution created enormous dislocations in the Chinese economy and society. From 1958 to 1978, per capita income stood still, while two thirds of the 200 billion yuan that the government invested in the economic supply was wasted.

The countryside was the worst hit. All those years, the annual income of the average peasant was just 76 yuan. More than 200 million farmers survived on a grain allotment of less than 331 pounds per year. A Cantonese farmer told me that for thirty years the Communists had not given them enough; he had a better life during the 1920s, when China was ruled by the warlords.

During the Cultural Revolution I was exiled to Xincai County in Henan Province. There, 36 percent of the people starved to death in the early 1960s.

The government decided what we should grow, the amount we should grow, and how much of it we should consume. Between 1949 and 1978, government investments in mechanical agriculture increased 16,000 times over, yet productivity in 1978 was lower than it was in 1956! Common sense says that any increase in mechanization should lead to a decrease in manpower. But in China, the increase in fixed investment and a 150 percent increase in manpower resulted in a decline in productivity. Farmers sometimes told us in private that even Chiang Kai-shek could have done a better job. As Communist officials, we felt wretched hearing this kind of talk.

—*Chen Yizi, a chief advisor of Zhao Ziyang*

Hai Diau Road, near Beijing University.

René Burri (Magnum)

what dormitory I lived in, and said that they were welcome to visit me any time. Everyone found this shocking, because at that time no one identified himself or risked linking his name with the movement. Immediately, I heard people saying: "What a man!" When I saw how backward China still was after forty years, when I saw what the Communist party had done to our people, I felt that we young people should take on some personal responsibility as well as a historical responsibility. Thoughts like these made me join the student movement.

—Wuer Kaixi

The student ringleaders were neither sincere nor consistent in conducting a dialogue. On April 18, Wang Dan and others demanded a dialogue with the People's Deputies from the National People's Congress (NPC),* which agreed immediately to their request. The students then said they didn't want any dialogue. Their sole demand was that repre-

sentatives from the NPC receive their petition outside of the Great Hall of People. Three hours later, however, more than 2,000 people tried to force their way into Xinhuamen.†

The student ringleaders gave several preconditions for the dialogue. They demanded that the government send only leading Politburo members, vice-premiers, or NPC deputies. They also specified that both sides had to agree on the time and location, and publish a joint communiqué. Their purpose was to force the government to recognize them as an equal political force, which, of course, we could not accept.

—Yuan Mu, former journalist; spokesman for the State Council since 1988

On April 19, five days after the death of Hu Yaobang, I called Professor Bao Zunxin. I told him that I saw a *dazibao* [a big-character poster] at People's University that was addressed to us. It said that not long ago there were many well-respected democracy advocates who lectured us

---

* The NPC meets once a year to approve decisions recommended by the CCP central committee.

† Xinhuamen, or "New China Gate," is the front entrance to Zhongnanhai, the central headquarters of the CCP and the official residence of China's top leaders.

(We) shared a universal aim to carry the demonstration to the end. I realized the strength of these people. We knew we were doing the right thing.

to fight for democracy. But when we finally stood up and marched in the streets, we could not find them. Bao and I felt we had to do something to respond to the challenge. We decided to write an open letter to the Party, the State, and the People's Congress.

Along with several other intellectuals (all of whom are now wanted by the government), we wrote the letter that night. This letter marked the first public support of students from intellectuals. The next day more than 200 well-known intellectuals signed it.

On the evening of April 21, three others and I went to the west entrance of Zhongnanhai to deliver the letter. We did not choose the front entrance—many students were holding a sit-in there, and we didn't want the government to lose face.

The guard refused to take our letter. He threw it on the floor. When we wanted to leave, the guards wouldn't let us. They took us inside and interrogated us for more than forty minutes. Only after they learned that many of the signatures were from members of the People's Congress did they begin to soften up. Finally, an officer came, but he also refused to take the letter. We were very angry, so we gave the letter to the Hong Kong press that night.

—Yuan Zhiming, graduate student in philosophy at People's University

On April 19, we were on our way to Xinhuamen when the police stopped us on Changan Avenue.* Three hundred of us were in front of Xinhuamen. Earlier, there had been a few thousand, but most of them had gone. I jumped on top of a bicycle cart and led the crowd; it was the first time that I actually stood up to lead. The police beat all of us, including me, but I hit back.

None of these several hundred people had known each other before, yet they were orderly and shared a universal aim to carry the demonstration through to the end. I was greatly encouraged, because I realized the strength of these people. We knew we were doing the right thing.

—Wuer Kaixi

On April 19, police clashed with students in front of Zhongnanhai. The Politburo met the next morning. At the meeting, Li Peng said, "I think the students were instigated by a small group of people and that this entire affair is aimed at the Party, especially the elderly leaders."

Zhao Ziyang responded, "There are so many people involved, it's doubtful that a 'small group' of people could have been behind it. I think we should be very cautious. We should try to solve the problem through dialogue."

—Chen Yizi

On April 21, the day before Hu Yaobang's funeral, I put up posters at every college campus in Beijing. They read: "The Beijing Provisional Student Union has now been established. The former Beijing Student Union and Graduate Student Union have been abolished. All students please attend an oath-taking rally at 9:00 P.M. at Beijing Normal University." Then I posted another poster at Beijing Normal University; this one read: "Those departments which have not yet registered, please register now. All students should obey the Provisional Student Union leadership. [Signed] Wuer Kaixi, Provisional Chairman." Actually, at that time, there were no departments registered at all, and the Provisional Student Union had only one member—me. I knew that the student movement had reached a critical point and that all it needed was one spark for it to catch fire. What I did was create that spark. This is one of the reasons why the Communist party resents me the most.

At 9:00 P.M. sharp, in front of 60,000 people, I climbed on top of a pair of parallel bars. The bars were shaking under my feet as I announced through a bullhorn, "Please be quiet." Then I declared that the Beijing Provisional Student Union was officially established. Thundering applause shook the air. I was thrilled but not scared. I hardly ever experience fear. I knew that every word I said was history, for it marked the emergence of the first independent self-governing political force in China. This organization was the precursor of the Beijing Autonomous Student Union.

After I finished speaking I looked down and saw my father standing below the parallel bars. This was one of the more despicable things that the government did. My father was in Beijing, at the Party school; they put enormous pressure on him to come find me and talk to me.

Actually, the Student Union wasn't officially constituted until three days after my declaration from the parallel bars, when leaders from all of the other schools held a secret meeting at Yuanmingyuan, the great ruined garden of the Manchu emperors. More than thirty people attended. At the meeting, the organization emerged, and the standing committee was selected.

On April 22, at the funeral of Hu Yaobang, three of the four student representatives got down on their knees in front of the Great Hall of the People—all except one, me. The three of them tried to force me to my knees, but I refused.

---

* Changan Avenue, or "Avenue of Eternal Peace," runs east-west through the center of Beijing.

At the main entrance to Zhongnanhai, a
woman begs students to end a sit-in.
Bill Pierce (Sygna)

THE DEATH OF HU YAOBANG
53

Thundering applause shook the air. I was thrilled but not scared. I hardly ever experience fear. I knew that every word I said was history.

Democracy is not something that you can beg for. There will never be democracy and freedom if you try to get them by begging. It's feudal to get down on our knees to our rulers. It's absurd; is it not ridiculous to fight for democracy and freedom by means of a feudal ritual?

Earlier that day, I had stood outside the Great Hall of the People and tearfully begged for a meeting with Li Peng. Seeing that tears achieved nothing, I grabbed a bullhorn and began to demand at the top of my lungs. I shouted for about one hour; I could see that most of the PLA [People's Liberation Army] soldiers in the front rows were moved to tears. I said that we simply wanted to talk, and I was totally carried away by my own sincerity. "Look," I said, intending my words for Li Peng. "So many students have starved for the whole day just for the opportunity to talk to you." I could see that many people inside the Great Hall were listening to me; many of the soldiers inside had lowered their heads. Then, many students, especially those from Beijing Normal University, began to move toward me and some of them kneeled.

I shouted, "After forty years of the People's Republic, this is the first time a man has stood under the national emblem, in front of the Great Hall, in front of the highest authority, and demanded a dialogue with you. I protest! You are shameless!"

The soldiers began to beat us when we tried to leave the steps of the Great Hall. They really beat us, too. When we were finally out of Tiananmen Square, I fainted from hunger and exhaustion.

—Wuer Kaixi

After Zhao Ziyang delivered the eulogy for Hu Yaobang, we filed past to pay our last respects. As we walked by the glass doors of the Great Hall of the People, many lingered for a moment to observe the many thousands of students sitting outside on the square. Rows of soldiers stood with arms linked to separate the students from us. I felt rage as I stood there silently watching them. The atmosphere was tense. Some of the officials feared that the students might try to force their way into the Great Hall. A soldier came over and asked me politely to move on.

My driver walked up to me and took my arm.

I replied, "I just want to stand here for a while. I belong to the Communist party, and I was wounded serving the Party during the war. I have seen much, but I have never before seen such abuse of students by Party members like yourself."

The soldier listened and then left. The incident inspired me to write a poem a little while later.

One land is split
By a wall of brute force.
On one side lies an iceberg, chilling those who dwell
    there.
And on the other a warm-water sea.
Here lies Yaobang's body,
And there his soul.
From there we all came;
If there is no "there" there wouldn't be any "here."

The next day, I showed the poem to the chief editor of the *Wen Hui* monthly in Shanghai. I asked him, "Will you dare to print this in your paper?"

He stopped reading when he saw the "wall of brute force," and shook his head.

—Ge Yang, chief editor of New Observer *magazine*

A speech given by Prof. Chen Mingyuan at Beijing University on April 23, 1989.

My name is Chen Mingyuan.
[Applause]
If someone wants to inform on me, he can give my name to the Public Security Bureau.*
[More applause]
I know that whenever students make reasonable requests or demands, whenever people become excited, there will always be a few who would like to betray their comrades, their friends, and even their own souls, in order to climb a few more rungs up the ladder.
[Applause]
I am forty-eight years old.† I am not afraid.

The first thing I want to say is that I attended Hu Yaobang's funeral yesterday. Throughout the service, I was very sad indeed. Hu Yaobang spoke a great deal about education, price control, intellectuals, and reform. . . .
[Applause]
At the end of the memorial service, several other comrades and I suggested that the hearse carrying Hu's body should circle Tiananmen Square, in keeping with convention. We should let Comrade Yaobang take one last look at the Monument to the People's Heroes and Tiananmen Gate. But the government refused. I was profoundly disappointed. I know that many comrades, many Chinese, were very disappointed. If Comrade

---

* The Public Security Bureau is the internal police force of China.
† This is a reference to Wen Yiduo, a well-known Chinese writer who died at age forty-seven.

April 23. Over 2,500 students listen
to the speech of Chen Mingyuan.
(Reuters)

Yaobang were still alive, he would feel very disappointed, too. We demand an official explanation for this unpopular decision. . . .

[Applause]

I have no wish to instigate trouble, and I have no ulterior motives. But our government, and our news media, have prepared a hat* for me nonetheless.

[Applause]

Under the present circumstances, people are terrified to stand up. Anyone who does stand up has to consider the safety of his parents, his children, and his job. Every month, he collects only a small salary. If he goes to jail, what will happen to his family? I have never stood up before so many people, but today I felt that I just could not stay silent. I have to speak out!

[Applause]

I want to protest strongly against official television. I have already called them and told them—through many different channels—that their reports on April 19 and April 20 were totally irresponsible. Did everyone here hear what was reported on CCTV?†

[Crowd: "Yes, we heard!"]

Did anyone in the demonstration shout antigovernment slogans?

[Crowd: "No!"]

Did CCTV say they did?

[Crowd: "Yes!"]

Did anyone put up antigovernment posters?

[Crowd: "No!"]

CCTV said that many unidentified bystanders were there inciting the crowds. I was one of them, but I am not "unidentified," because at the beginning of this speech I told you my name. I think the one who incited the crowds was CCTV. And where is the person who wrote those broadcasts? He should stand up here!

[Crowd: "Yes!"]

He is the one who cannot be identified! He is the one who incited us!

[Laughter]

I think these recent student demonstrations were totally spontaneous. Nobody was behind them.

[Applause]

The demonstration was spontaneous, the petition peaceful, and the mourning of Comrade Yaobang very orderly. I think the students from Beijing University should feel very proud of themselves.

[Crowd: "Long live the students! Long live democracy! Long live freedom!" Applause]

When I pronounced the word "freedom," some people became nervous. Some would say, "Freedom is a

---

* In other words, a political label. Hats were used by the government during the Cultural Revolution to single out "counterrevolutionaries."
† CCTV, Chinese Central Television, is China's state-controlled television network.

A statue in front of Mao's mausoleum affords
an excellent view of the square.
Peter Wang

bad word." Some would say, "We should try to avoid using that word." But I feel that freedom is the most beautiful word in the world. Why should only other people be allowed to use it? Why is it that this beautiful word is not in the vocabulary of our great motherland and our great people?

[Applause]

Yes, we are poor. We are backward. We are undereducated. We are living a bitter life. But we do have this ideal of freedom and democracy. . . .

[Applause]

Many of us are afraid of press freedom. Whenever we talk about the freedom of the press, someone says that "something will go wrong"; they say that we shouldn't publicize our "family scandals." But I believe that truth is the soul of the media. . . .

[Cheers and applause]

Those who ignored the students' demands—which came from the bottom of their hearts—should ask themselves why they are afraid of the students. . . .

[Long applause]

If you ask all our comrades, "What is the most severe problem in our reforms?" they will say, "inflation." What is the *real* inflation rate? The government told us it was 18 percent. I work every day. I do household chores. I shop and buy groceries. But I can't even afford to buy new clothes! Pork used to cost eighty fen a pound. Now it's up to four or five yuan. In Canton, it has even reached ten yuan. . . .*

When we come to the problem of education, every one of us has spoken about it until our lips have cracked. Why can't we make education a top priority on the list of government expenditures?

[Crowd: "Yes!" Applause]

The government has always told us that this is too difficult, that there's a shortage of funds in industry, that there's a shortage of money in agriculture. It's even very difficult to build houses for all those mayors and governors. But I think that there's one thing that should not be so difficult. That is to confiscate the illegal income from the racketeers and spend *that* on education!

[Applause]

Students, I'm very troubled these days. There are so many problems in our country today. But the issues we raised here are the most basic ones. . . .

We are the masters of our country.

[Crowd: "Yes!" Long applause]

Meanwhile we have to report truthfully on those corrupt government officials, no matter how high up they may be, and punish them according to law.

[Crowd: "Yes! Well said!"]

Maybe someone will say, "You students should

---

* There are 100 fen per yuan, China's official currency. $1 U.S. = 3.7 yuan.

Wuer Kaixi and student demonstrators break a police blockade, May 4.
Ken Wong (K & W)

"I have good feelings for the Party. I grew up from a peasant boy into a doctor thanks to the Communists." "I don't believe in the Communist party," I replied.

return and study quietly. You professors should simply teach your courses." But all these problems constantly wear us down. We can't accept this. We shall never accept it!

Deng Xiaoping's April 24 speech before the mayor of Beijing, the basis of the April 26 *People's Daily* editorial condemning the student movement.

This is no ordinary student movement: This is turmoil. We must take a clear stand, adopt effective measures, and not let them succeed in their aim. These people have been influenced by the liberals of Yugoslavia, Poland, Hungary, and the Soviet Union. Their aim is to overthrow the Communist government and make the future bleak for China. We must act swiftly. We should not be afraid of others cursing our mothers, or of international reaction. There can only be true democracy when China is developed and modernized.

The Four Cardinal Principles* are absolutely necessary. Comrade Hu Yaobang was too weak, and failed to carry them out. He quit the Anti–Spiritual Pollution movement only twenty days after it had begun. If he had persisted, turmoil such as this would never have occurred.

Among the four principles, there is one calling for upholding the people's democratic dictatorship. We now need to implement this principle. Of course, we shall do so properly.

The turmoil must not reach the high schools—it is important to maintain stability there. They will incite the younger students to make trouble. The workers are stable, but there is some potential for instability. The peasants present no problem. . . .

This turmoil is a planned conspiracy. These people want to destroy China's bright future. Their targets are the Party's leadership and the socialist system.

Dialogue with them is possible, but it must be conducted properly. Otherwise, it would only fuel their egos. We must avoid bloodshed, but it may not be possible to avoid it entirely.

The turmoil now at hand is nationwide and must not be underestimated. We shall publish a strong editorial and strive to strengthen legislation. Unfortunately, we

have lost much time. Now they are using their constitutional rights to struggle against us. But we have Ten Regulations in Beijing that we will use to contain them. We must prepare for a nationwide struggle, and suppress this turmoil. Otherwise, there will be no peace under heaven. I told [George] Bush that if China permitted demonstrations, with so many people, it would be far too chaotic. We could never get anything done.

They are using the same old tactics used by troublemakers during the Cultural Revolution. If they succeed, all the work we have done toward reform will come to a halt, almost overnight.

Now, 60,000 students are boycotting classes in Beijing, while 100,000 are not. We should support these 100,000 and win over most of the other 60,000. The workers, the peasants, and the cadres all support us. The other parties existing under our system are good, too. And we have several million PLA soldiers!

Comrade Yaobang made mistakes, but now that he is dead we speak of his good side. . . . He did many good things, such as supporting the reforms, but this does not mean that he is without mistakes. He was weak and yielded to the bourgeois liberal trend. His economic policies were also wrong. If we had adopted his plan, inflation would be much worse than it is now. The honor given to his memorial service was more than sufficient. Some people wanted us to call him a "Great Marxist." None of deserve that honor. You should not use it for me when I am dead.

We must quickly put an end to this turmoil. The more the Poles gave in, the greater their turmoil became. The opposition is very powerful in Poland, and there is Solidarity.

In the past, we have not sufficiently emphasized the Four Cardinal Principles and adherence to the people's democratic dictatorship. We cannot do without them. Have they not come in handy now?

I was in the hospital on the night of April 25. When I heard the *People's Daily* editorial on the radio, I knew everything had gone wrong. I immediately called several leaders and told them that if the government tried to persecute some of the student leaders, it was the Party that would really suffer most of all. I said that if that happened, China would be in for a period of serious turmoil. Some of them agreed with me; others told me that I was being simplistic.

—Chen Yizi

*The Four Cardinal Principles, articulated by Deng Xiaopeng, include: upholding Socialist principles, People's Democratic Dictatorship, CCP leadership, and Marxist-Leninist-Maoist thought.

Changan Avenue.
Kenneth Jarecke
(Contact Press Images)

The Beijing Student Union met again on April 25. During that meeting, the government-controlled radio broadcast the infamous *People's Daily* editorial condemning the student movement as "turmoil" aimed at overthrowing the government. I pressed for a rally and advocated marching on the twenty-seventh. After heated debate, my proposal was passed by a vote of about twenty-five to fifteen. The next day, the authorities put tremendous pressure on the various schools to repudiate the march. But march we did. We broke through every police barrier peacefully; we gave them no excuse to use force or to criticize us later. This is why the officials had such a headache over us.

— *Wuer Kaixi*

On the night of April 26 we heard that troops had been called into Beijing. In this tense atmosphere, some of us decided that we should try to stop the students.

That night we biked to Beijing University and found the campus packed with people—a warm atmosphere that completely dispelled our worries. The preparatory committee was voting on whether to march the next day. Everything was being decided democratically; a majority of students voted to demonstrate, and we saw that we had no right to stop them from doing so. Forgetting that we were there to dissuade the students from protesting, we sang along with them: "Beijing U., Beijing U., people fostered you; unafraid of pressure, unafraid of blood . . ." It was the song we were going to sing in the demonstration the next day; we went home humming it.

The next morning, there were police everywhere. I was to chair a scholarly meeting at the Institute of Literary Research; I was hardly in the mood for academics but had no way to cancel it. When we gathered, it was obvious that no one wanted to discuss literature. So we decided to go talk to the students again.

I cycled to the Chinese Academy of Social Sciences through streets filled with police.* At each intersection we tried to persuade the students to turn around. By the time I reached Tiananmen Square it had been completely sealed off. I went immediately to Xidan,† where I saw Wuer Kaixi leading the procession. People carried him on their shoulders as they pushed past the police. In the distance I heard civil-

---

* The main branch of the Chinese Academy of Social Sciences (CASS) is on Jianguomen-wai Avenue, about two miles east of Tiananmen Square.
† Xidan is a major shopping street one mile west of Tiananmen.

ians shouting "No beating! No beating!" More than ten lines of police blocked the avenue; people shouted and jumped for joy as the students broke through the blockade. Changan Avenue was totally packed.

The demonstration lasted until midnight. I was among the thousands of civilians who gathered in the western suburbs to applaud the students' triumphant return. We handed out heaps of food, candies, and fruits to them. Quite literally shedding tears of joy, many teachers—including senior professors and university presidents—embraced the students at the gates of the schools.

The April 27 demonstration was an explosion of all the energy that had accumulated over the past ten years. In those few days, the spirit of the Chinese people was at its height, and the huge façade of authority that the Communist party had been erecting for decades began to crack.

—Su Wei, a leading Chinese critic

April 27 symbolized the beginning of the end of Deng Xiaoping's power. On the morning of April 26, the Chinese Democratic League* had held a meeting to request that the Chinese government not use force against the students. Yan Mingfu conveyed the request to the Central Committee, and there was no crackdown on April 27. The success of that meeting gave the intellectuals a feeling of power.

—Yan Jiaqi, former director of the Political Science Institute at the Chinese Academy of Social Sciences

On April 29, Zhao Ziyang returned from North Korea and held a Politburo meeting that included Yang Shangkun and Wan Li. Zhao referred to the widespread discontent among the people and argued that the main problem was official corruption. He made several suggestions: first, to disclose the results of the investigations into companies accused of official racketeering; second, to close the luxury stores that were only open to high-ranking officials; third, to set up a supervisory committee to monitor officials and their children's financial activities; and fourth, to complete the legislation governing the freedom of the press as soon as possible. Zhao also wanted these proposals published in the press to demonstrate official sincerity. Wan Li immediately agreed. But Li Peng stood against it.

—Chen Yizi

My father came to Beijing on May Day. He loves me very much. Because I had some disputes with my husband, I went alone on my last trip home. He was very concerned. When my father came he brought all kinds of treats for us and hoped we would all spend some time together.

The Provisional Student Union called for an end to the boycott of classes on May 4.

After he arrived, though, he found us deeply involved in this movement and was quite worried. We had little time to spend with him.

One night he told me, "I have to go home. I can't really help you in any way here. Please, stay in touch."

I told him I would send him a telegram every three days, and I did ask a friend to do this.

"What if I don't receive your telegrams?" he asked.

I said, "Don't come back then. There would be nothing you could do." I almost fell into his arms and burst out crying. But he calmed me and said, "Don't cry when we say farewell." Then he said good-bye.

My father is a very strong man and an ambitious doctor. His generation has its own hopes and needs. But for the past few years, all this hope has been missing. People have lost their faith, their only concern being money. I knew my father was very depressed. I empathized with him. He told me, "I still have good feelings for the Party. I grew up from a

---

* A Chinese political party officially recognized by the CCP.

Gabriel (VU)

On May 1, Fei Xiaotong called for a congress of Beijing intellectuals. He was afraid that the students would demonstrate again on May 4. The meeting was chaired by Li Zehou. Twenty renowned intellectuals attended the meeting, and everyone felt that they should appeal to the Chinese government against the use of force. They favored a dialogue to alleviate the situation. I delivered a speech at the meeting in which I listed Deng Xiaoping's three serious mistakes: first, the Anti–Bourgeois Liberalization campaign, which led to the fall of Hu Yaobang; second, arbitrary moves in price reform; third, the April 26 editorial in the *People's Daily,* which had aroused widespread indignation. "Besides," I argued, "since Deng was neither a member of the Central Committee nor a member of the Politburo, why should the Central Committee listen to his every word?" I think that speech was reported to the government.

—Yan Jiaqi

peasant boy into a doctor thanks to the Communist party."

"I don't believe in the Communist party," I replied. "The Party has manipulated your generation. You should be getting so much more."

My father could understand me. "You haven't gone through what we have gone through," he said. "But you can have your own way of thinking."

My father spent many painstaking years raising two daughters. Now we are both irreversibly involved in the movement. I really feel bad for him. Whenever something happened to our family, my father has always been our only support. He has placed all his hopes on us. I want to continue living for him. But I know that the government will take severe actions against us, because Chinese people are vindictive. I have no illusions.

—Chai Ling, a student at Beijing Normal University; named commander in chief of the Tiananmen demonstrators

On May 4, student leaders announced a declaration that marked the beginning of a new democratic enlightenment movement. So it surprised everyone when a director of the Beijing Student Union proclaimed that the boycotting of classes was over and students would return to school the next day. Many students were very disappointed. This announcement seriously damaged the nationwide student movement. Someone said, "A million-dollar opportunity was ruined by a single decision."

Later, the movement dwindled to a low point as more and more students returned to classes. We wasted a lot of energy arguing whether or not to resume our classes. The situation became increasingly difficult.

At that point, we decided that we had to stage a hunger strike. Some from the Student Union were very much against this, but we persisted. We had been contemplating a hunger strike for some time. Marching and boycotting classes had drawn no response from the government.

—Chai Ling

THE DEATH OF HU YAOBANG

GER STRIKE

The hunger strike, which started on May 13, was initiated by six people, including Wang Dan, Ma Shaofang, myself, and three others. We first came up with the idea around May 8 or 9, and on May 10 we decided to go ahead with it. We held a meeting in a small, shabby, two-table restaurant. After the meeting, we put our money together—a total of twenty yuan—and had a meal. Our call for a strike was immediately answered by Beijing University, Beijing Normal University, the University of Politics and Law, and other schools.

—Wuer Kaixi

By the next day, more than 200 people had signed up for the hunger strike. We took a solemn oath and wore red headbands. We wrote "Democracy" and "Hunger strike" on the fronts of our shirts and the huge character *ai* [sad] on the backs. Some of the slogans read, "We have the hearts to serve the country, but we have no power to restore the heavenly order." We also wrote a hunger-strike declaration. To prepare us for the strike, many professors invited us to dinners; some even ordered special dumplings from distant places for us. I felt terribly sad that evening and couldn't eat anything. I said, "We shall fight to live even if it means we must assume a willingness to die."

At 12:30 P.M. the next day, all the hunger-strikers converged at Beijing Normal University and began marching to the square. We were laying down our lives to test the govern-

A hunger-striker faces soldiers in front of Zhongnanhai.
Kenneth Jarecke (Contact Press Images)

ment's intentions. The first night we had fewer than 1,000 participants. But by the end we had more than 3,000 hunger-strikers. Since I was one of the initiators, I felt the heavy burden of responsibility.

That same night, Wuer Kaixi and several others were called in by Yan Mingfu. Because of Gorbachev's visit, Yan requested that the hunger-strikers move to a different location. We agreed, reluctantly, to move. I felt that Wuer Kaixi was softened by Yan's father image.

—*Chai Ling*

The May 13 Hunger Strike Declaration

In these bright and beautiful days of May, we are beginning a hunger strike. We are young, but we are ready to give up our lives. We cherish life; we do not want to die.

But this nation is in a critical state. It suffers from skyrocketing inflation, growing crime rates, official profiteering, and other forms of bureaucratic corruption, concentration of power in a few people's hands, and the loss of a large number

Hunger-striker.   *Kenneth Jarecke (Contact Press Images)*

The poster applauds glasnost.
Kenneth Jarecke (Contact Press Images)

Deng Xiaoping meets Mikhail Gorbachev, the first USSR–China summit since 1959.

Kenneth Jarecke (Contact Press Images)

of intellectuals who would now rather stay overseas. At this life-and-death moment of the nation's fate, countrymen, please listen to us!

China is our motherland.

We are the people.

The government should be our government.

Who should speak out, if we should not?

Who should act, if we should not?

Although our bones are still forming, although we are too young for death, we are ready to leave you. We must go; we are answering the call of Chinese history.

Our honest feelings of patriotism and loyalty to the nation were distorted as "turmoil," and we were accused of being the tools of a "handful" who have "ulterior motives."

We ask of every Chinese citizen—every worker, peasant, soldier, civilian, celebrity, every government official, policeman, and our accusers—that you place your hand on your heart and ask yourself: What wrong have we done? What "turmoil" have we created? What causes have led us to protest, to demonstrate, to boycott classes, to fast, to hide ourselves? Why did this happen? Our words were not heard in good faith. We were beaten by police when we marched, though we were only hungry for the truth. Our representatives

knelt for hours, presenting our petition, only to be ignored by the government. Our request for dialogue has been put off again and again. The safety of our student leaders is now uncertain.

What shall we do?

Democracy is supposed to be the highest of human aspirations and freedom a sacred human right, granted at birth. Today these must be bought with our lives.

We say to our dear mothers and fathers, do not feel sorry for us when we are hungry. To our uncles and aunts, do not feel sad when we leave this life. We have one wish, that the lives of everyone we leave be better. We have one request, that you remember this: our pursuit is life, not death. Democracy is not a task for a few; it takes generations.

May this declaration, written with our lives, break up the clouds that cast their shadows on the People's Republic of China. We are doing this:

1. To protest the government's indifference to the student demonstrations;
2. To protest the government's failure to enter into a dialogue with students;

Outside the Great Hall of the People.
Kenneth Jarecke
(Contact Press Images)

In these bright and beautiful days, we are beginning a hunger strike. We are young, but are ready to give up our lives. We cherish life; we do not want to die.

3. To protest the government's unfair characterization of the student democratic movement as "turmoil" and the further distortion of it in newspaper coverage.

We request:

1. An immediate dialogue between the government and the students on substantial topics with equal status;
2. An acknowledgment by the government of the legitimacy of the student democratic movement.

Time of the hunger strike: Begins at 2:00 P.M., May 13, 1989.
Place of the hunger strike: Tiananmen Square.
—The hunger-strike volunteers

Some students, already weakened by the fast, had to be carried to the new location. We were surrounded by spectators. Later a student told me, "If the government keeps ignoring us, we'll have to resort to extreme action. If they are willing to see the students die, we hunger-strikers will be the first to sacrifice ourselves."

I announced on the PA system, "Since I am in charge of the hunger strike, I shall be the first to give up my life." Many hunger-strikers had also said that they were ready to die so that other students might live.

—Chai Ling

We decided to organize our own demonstration on May 15. This would be the first time during this movement that the intellectuals had taken to the streets. Someone suggested that we should march in silence and play funeral music instead of shouting slogans.

Camped out on the square. Spring is the rainy season in Beijing.

Kenneth Jarecke (Contact Press Images)

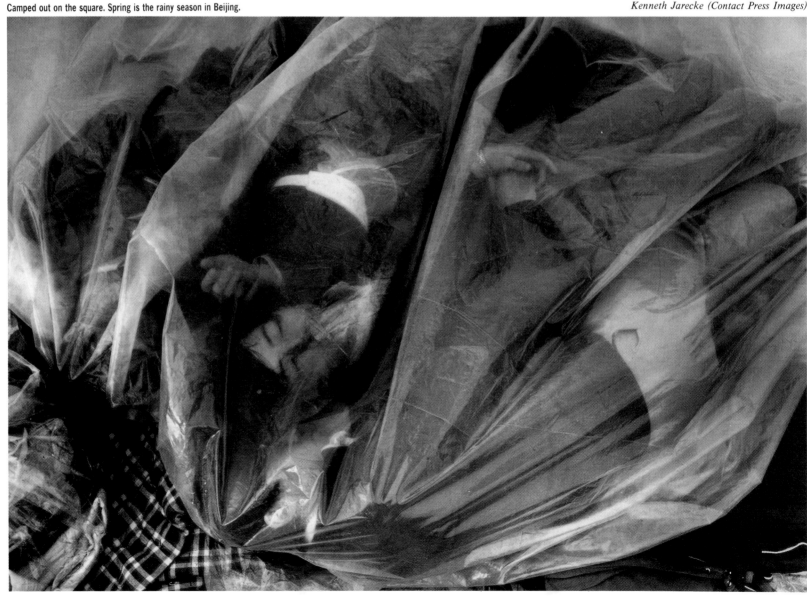

A quiet moment on the square.

Manuel Vimenet (VU)

After the meeting was over, Su Xiaokang, Bao Zunxin, and Zheng Yi went to Yan Jiaqi's home to consult with him on the draft of our declaration. Its original title was The May Declaration of the Intellectuals. Yan Jiaqi, however, argued that it should be named the May 16 Declaration, as a counterpart to the 1966 May 16 Notice, which marked the beginning of the Cultural Revolution; the May 16 Declaration of 1989 would mark the beginning of another era. After looking at it again, I changed the last phrase from "Long live the great socialist motherland" to "Long live a free and democratic China!" How many people would consider themselves Socialists now? I did not think I was one, at least.

On May 13, Dai Qing called and said, "Hu Qili agreed to meet with some of the intellectuals and listen to their views." The next day, twelve of us went to the *Guangming Daily* for the meeting. Dai Qing brought along Wang Chaohua, a student leader, to talk about the situation of the student movement. She said that the Beijing Autonomous Student Union had lost control of the square. Dai Qing had gotten news that the Soviet Embassy had notified the Chinese government that when Gorbachev arrived in Beijing the next day, Tiananmen Square must be cleared.

Wang Chaohua told us that only we, respected scholars, may exert any influence over the students. "We are useless," she claimed. At the same time, Yan Mingfu, the minister of the United Front,* called saying that their dialogue with the students had collapsed, and that tens of thousands of students were surrounding the ministry. He wanted us to come there and help hold off the siege.

Yan Jiaqi insisted that there must be a few preconditions for the students to evacuate the square: particularly, the government must show goodwill in conducting a dialogue with the students. Wen Yuankai and a few others maintained that the government should be allowed to save face. That made me angry; this was not a matter of face. If we were going to ask the students to leave the square, it was the government that had to make a gesture.

Yan Jiaqi said that our stand was quite clear; that we supported the students and we were going to protect them;

---

* The Ministry of the United Front is the department of the Chinese government that handles relations with overseas Chinese, particularly those in Taiwan and Hong Kong.

Hei Bai (VU)

Li Zehou turned around and said, "I suppose this is how history is written; we're powerless, and are being pushed into the streets by the force of events."

we were not mediators for the government. If the government refused to meet these demands, we would stand with the students.

We met Wuer Kaixi at the Ministry of the United Front. He also told us that the Student Union had lost control, and he hoped that we would help get the students out of the ministry. There may have been 20,000 to 30,000 people there. When we introduced ourselves, the students cheered. Dai Qing then read our declaration, and we led the students directly to Tiananmen Square. I was very excited, feeling that we were participating in a great historic moment. But I also felt ridiculous. Who were we, after all? Li Zehou, who had been observing the crowds on both sides, suddenly turned around and said, with an ironic smile, "I suppose this is how history is written; we're completely powerless and are being pushed into the streets by the force of events."

At the square we gave speeches. On the one hand, we took the side of the students; on the other, we tried to persuade them to leave. Without conferring with us, Dai Qing

told the students, "The twelve of us have contacted the central government; if you agree to leave, we will get Zhao Ziyang and Hu Qili to come to the square to meet you, but you may not ask questions. Then all of us can leave the square." The students objected. All of a sudden the square was thrown into chaos. Our group was pushed out of the square feeling betrayed by Dai Qing because she had not consulted us.

—*Su Wei*

The May 16 Declaration

In the minds of the Chinese people, the "May 16 Notice" of 1966 was undoubtedly a symbol of tyranny and darkness. Today, twenty-three years later, we strongly sense the call of democracy and a bright future. A patriotic and democratic movement with the students in the vanguard is emerging

Hunger-strikers, Changan Avenue.

Kenneth Jarecke (Contact Press Images)

The Politburo met at Deng Xiaoping's home on May 17. Zhao Ziyang suggested two ways to resolve the student problem, a "soft" solution and a "tough" one.

throughout the nation. . . . This is a great, historic turning point that will determine the fate of China. . . .

At this decisive moment, we—the mainland and overseas Chinese intellectuals—have chosen this day, May 16, 1989, to sign the declaration below, which openly articulates our principles and positions:

1. It is our view that actions taken by certain government and Party leaders have been unwise with regard to the current student movement. Not long ago there were indications from the government that force would be used to deal with the student movement. It is worthwhile to reflect on the lessons of history: the Beijing government of 1919, the Kuomintang government of the 1930s and 1940s, the Gang of Four of the late 1970s and other dictatorships, all used violence to suppress student movements. Without exception, those who were responsible were labeled "historical disgraces." History proves: suppressors of student movements come to no good end. Were the rules of modern democratic politics applied, the will of the people respected, and current trends followed, a democratic

and stable China would emerge. Otherwise, a China full of hope will be drawn into an abyss of great turmoil.

2. The unavoidable first step in handling the present political crisis democratically is the recognition of the legality of the autonomous student organizations, which were created through a democratic process. If not, it would be a violation of the provision of freedom of assembly set forth in the constitution. Branding student organizations as illegal would only intensify the conflict and aggravate the crisis.

3. The direct cause of this political crisis is the phenomenon of corruption, which the young students have spoken out against so strongly during this movement. The greatest mistake of the past ten years is a neglect to reform the political structure. . . . The leaders should respect the demands of the people, promote systematic political reform, put an end to special privilege, investigate and ban "official racketeering," and eliminate corruption.

4. During the student movement, news organs, such as Xinhua News Agency and the People's Daily, concealed the

An emergency tent aids the weak and exhausted. Most of the young women are medical students.

Kenneth Jarecke (Contact Press Images)

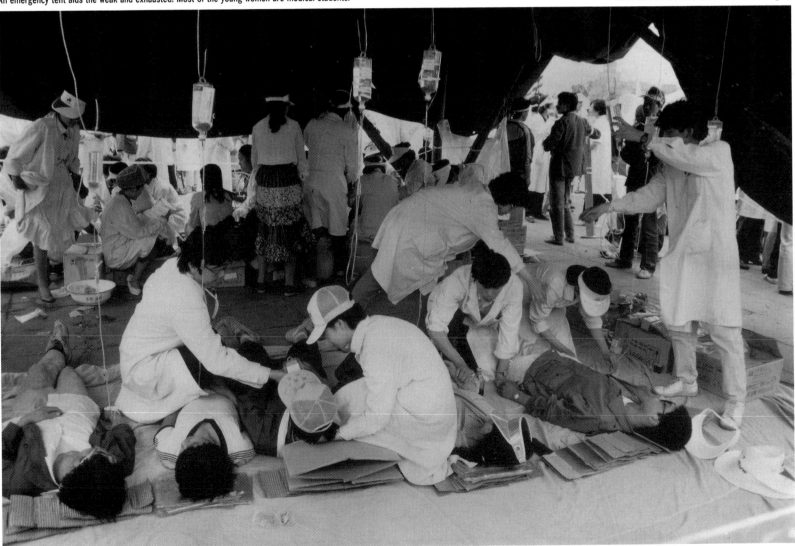

Jacques Langevin (Sygma)

How do you feel about the hunger strikers? a. Support them (277); b. Understand them (193); c. Don't understand them (17); d. Don't care (0).

facts, depriving people of their right to know; the Shanghai Municipal Committee of the Chinese Communist Party suspended the duties of Qin Benli, editor in chief of the World Economic Herald. *These erroneous actions represent an utter disregard for our constitution. Freedom of the press is an effective method of routing out corruption, maintaining national stability, and promoting social development. Absolute power that is not subject to supervision inevitably leads to absolute corruption. When freedom of the press is not put into effect, if the people are not allowed to establish and run newspapers, then all of the wishes and promises concerning liberalization and reform will result in nothing more than a blank sheet of paper.*

5. It is wrong to call this student movement an anti-Party, anti-Socialist political insurrection. The fundamental meaning of freedom of speech is to acknowledge and even protect the citizen's right to express different political views. The essence of the various political movements since liberation—the Anti–Hu Feng movement, the Anti-Rightist movement, the Cultural Revolution, the Anti–Spiritual Pollution movement, and Anti–Bourgeois Liberalization compaign—has been to put pressure on and attack different political views. A society with only one voice is inherently unstable. It is necessary for the Party and the government to review the profound lessons of these movements. Opening all channels of speech, consulting with students, intellectuals, and all people on affairs of state is the only possible way to create a real, stable, and unified political system.

6. The idea of "a handful of" or of "long beard" backstage manipulators* is wrong. Regardless of age, all citizens of the People's Republic of China hold an equal political position and have the right to participate and to discuss politics. Freedom, democracy, and legality have never been granted. All the people who pursue truth and love should make untiring efforts to attain freedom of thought, of speech, and of the press and the right to gather, organize, march, and demonstrate, which are guaranteed to every citizen by our constitution.

* Refers to the older intellectuals who the government blames for instigating the demonstration and hunger strike.

Cadets from the police academy.

Ken Wong (K & W)

Our nation has no time to lose and can no longer turn back.

Chinese intellectuals, you are full of patriotism and conscience. Realize your unshirkable historic responsibility and stand out to advocate the democratic process. Fight for establishing a modern nation with political democracy and a flourishing economy!

Long live the people!

Long live a free and democratic China!

The Politburo met at Deng Xiaoping's home on May 17. Zhao Ziyang suggested two ways to resolve the student problem, a "soft" solution and a "tough" one. The "soft" solution would be to recognize the student movement as patriotic and their organization as legitimate. The "tough" solution would be to declare martial law. In the short run, martial law might pacify the situation, but in the long run, it would also create endless new problems.

—Chen Yizi

At the beginning we were united. But by the third day, after seeing many of our fellow hunger-strikers being carried away in ambulances, some of the students, along with some Beijing residents, wanted to force their way into the Great Hall of the People. At that point we didn't have enough student guards. I had to ask the hunger-strikers to form a human wall to protect the Great Hall. Standing between police and the angry crowd, we shouted to the crowd, "If you want to force your way into the Great Hall, you will have to step over our bodies."

The leaders of the hunger strike held a meeting with the Autonomous Student Union and requested that control of the square be given to us. During that period all kinds of student organizations had sprung up. Anyone could form an organization and change its leaders at will. Student leaders from various organizations formed territories and proclaimed themselves commanders. In the Beijing Autonomous Student Union alone there had been no fewer than 182 changes in the chairmanship. The handling of donations had become very messy.

Furthermore, sanitary conditions in the square were

The Beijing transit system donated the use of over eighty giant busses.

Patrick Zachmann (Magnum)

getting worse and worse, and we feared it would cause some disease epidemic. The students were becoming agitated and tempers flared. All kinds of rumors spread among us. One minute we would think that the army was being sent to crush us, the next minute it was something else.

The confusion in the square helped Li Peng gain precious time, which he used to convince six military regions to support him. Zhao Ziyang and his people gradually lost their power. Yan Mingfu was certainly out of the picture. I knew little about such internal power struggles.

In the eyes of the students, the government was heartless. Morale was dropping, disillusionment grew, and the students didn't know what they wanted anymore or what to do next. Some students left, feeling only remorse. Others filled their own pockets with the contributions and went off to spend what they stole.

Even worse, some students were lured away by the government with promises of heroic honors if they helped convince the other students to withdraw. I myself was approached by some of these students. During our conversations they dropped hints that those who persuaded students to withdraw would be treated "fairly."

—*Chai Ling*

The early morning of May 16, the third day of fasting.
Patrick Zachmann (Magnum)

Among the 3,000 strikers there were between 7,000 and 8,000 cases of people passing out. I had been taken to the hospital more than ten times. I stopped my fast on the fifth day.

At one point my heart stopped beating. I may have had heart problems before but never knew it. After a sudden sharp pain, everything went dark, and I fell over unconscious. I woke up later in the hospital. By the fifth day I was running a high fever, and the doctors all wept while trying to get me to eat.

Of course, every hunger-striker suffered one kind of breakdown or another. Some of my friends were in really bad condition: their gums, faces, and lips were all bloodless, deathly pale.

—*Wuer Kaixi*

An account of the hunger strike from the *Beijing Youth Newspaper*, May 18, 1989

The sun rose blood-red the morning of May 17, awakening the weakened hunger-strikers. The shrill sirens of ambulances pierced the hearts of Beijing citizens.

On the evening of May 16, following the advice of Comrade Yan Mingfu after his visit to the square, three groups—the Beijing Student Hunger-Strike Petition Committee, the Beijing Student Dialogue Representative Committee, and the Beijing Autonomous Student Union—called a meeting. After an hour-long debate, the latter two groups agreed to give the government "more time," to clear the square, and to sign a document of agreement. A survey of hunger-striking students taken by the Hunger-Strike Committee, however, indicated that 2,699 students (95 percent of all students present) opposed the pullout, while only 54 students were willing to leave. The two groups proposing the pullout agreed to the wishes of the hunger-striking students and decided not to leave the square.

As for the press, reporters were folding newspapers into hats and wearing them. A China Daily *banner reading "A certain tree in China blooms once in 40 years; Party journalists want to speak the truth" caused a commotion.*

Workers shouted: "It hurts us to see these students hungry—we're not afraid of being fired, nor do we want our salaries or bonuses."

The students' central headquarters.

David C. Turnley (Black Star)

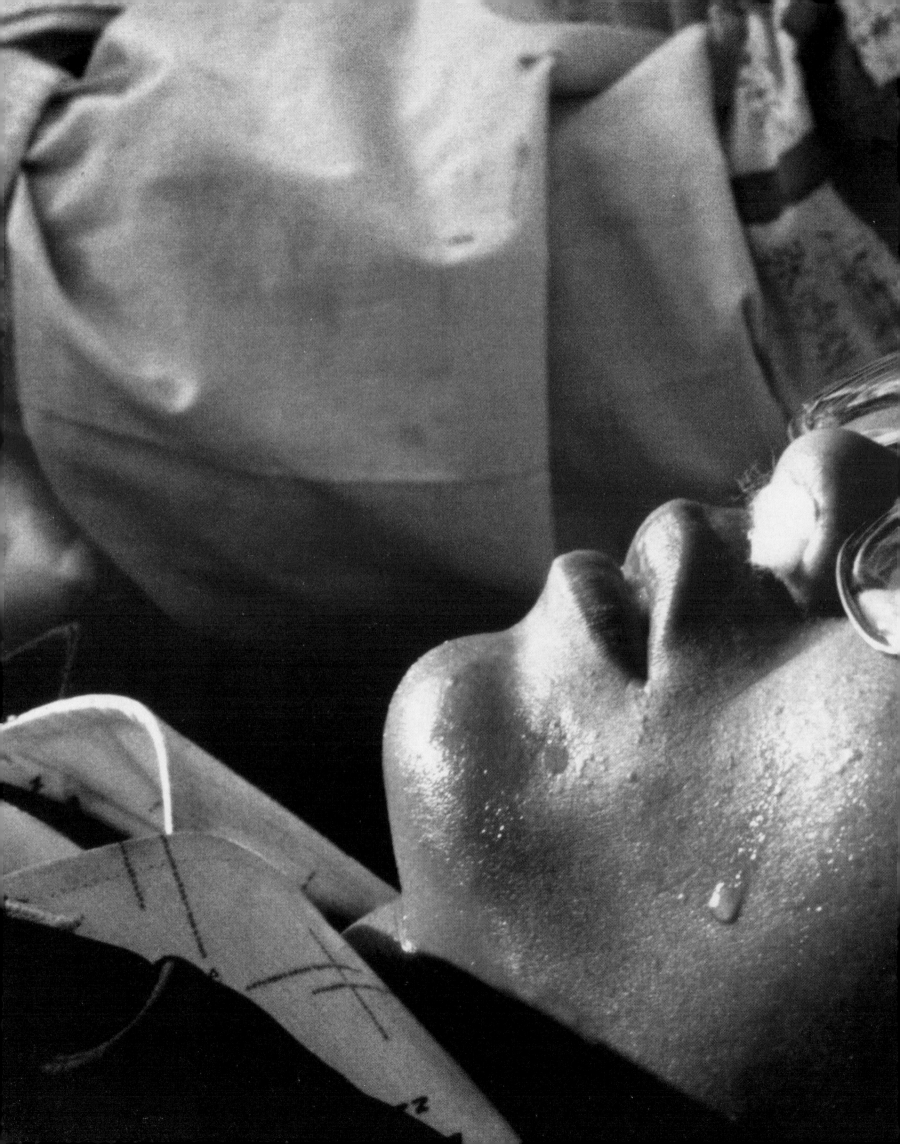

Kenneth Jarecke (Contact Press Images)

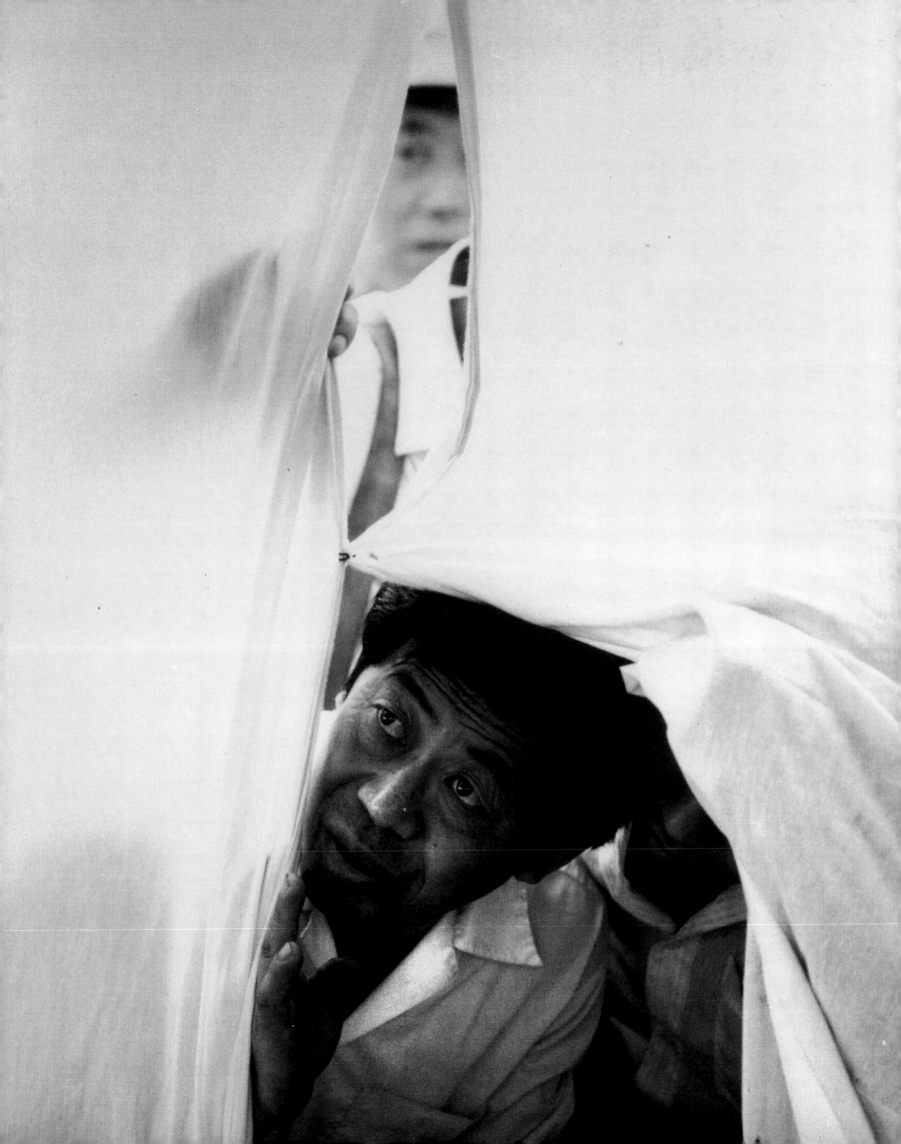

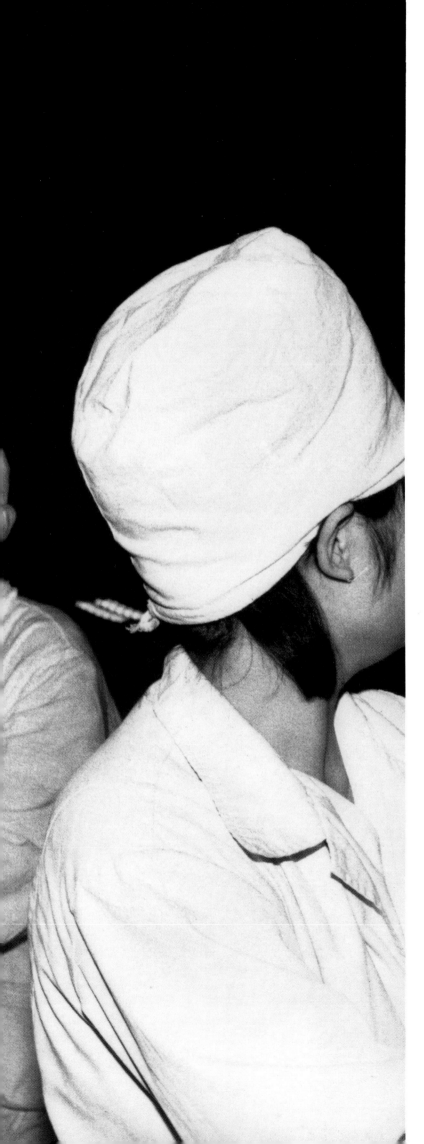

A banner from the National Women's Federation of China read: "Young students risking their lives; we mothers cannot just look on."

Elementary school students, wearing Young Pioneers scarves, waved small flags imploring "Save our big brothers and sisters."

Banners held by doctors and nurses read: "Corruption + Decadence = Cancer."

Nearly one million demonstrated, representing various communities: government, education, the arts, and business—both private and state owned.

Around 10:40 P.M., a group dressed in police uniforms entered the square carrying a large banner: "The People's Public Security University of China." Following them was a smaller banner: "We Have Arrived."

At around 3:00 P.M. a reporter at the intersection of Qianmen Street saw a student guiding a vehicle with a flag through the crowd. A large crowd of students walking hand in hand quickly dropped their banner and parted to both sides of the road, clearing a wide path among the thousands of bobbing heads. People darted to either side, forming a human wall to let the ambulance pass safely.

The fact that over a thousand of these students voluntarily and spontaneously organized themselves so well was the lifeline of this movement.

A student from Hefei University [in Anhui Province], who remained on the east side of the square all day, said that the Beijing students were very resourceful, and that he had come on his own accord to help out. A traffic policeman who wished to remain anonymous said that this was the first time in his twenty-plus years of service that he had seen civilians directing traffic.

May 18. Li Peng visits Xiehe Hospital. *(Gamma/Xinhua)*

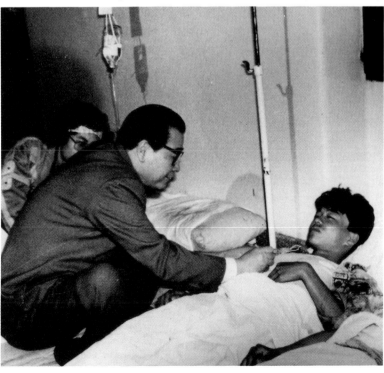

Being rushed to a nearby hospital.
Patrick Zachmann (Magnum)

Freedom of speech . . . acknowledges the citizen's right to express different political views. A society with only one voice is inherently unstable.

Nine-twenty P.M. on May 16 marked the one hundredth hour of the hunger strike. By that time, more than 1,400 students had passed out. The students had set up a special access road to accommodate the nonstop stream of ambulances. Most of the hunger-strikers lay under plastic tarps or inside tents.

At the hunger-strike headquarters, a reporter saw one of the hunger-strike leaders, wearing a hospital gown, surrounded by several doctors and nurses, who urged him to return to the hospital. This was the sixth time he had left the hospital without their consent. He had first passed out on the morning of May 15 when he had urged students from People's University to move to the east side of the square so as not to interfere with the ceremonies welcoming Gorbachev.

Now he was concerned about the future of the hunger strike. So many students, far above the expected number, had

turned out. If the government did not do something to satisfy the demands of the students, he felt things would be worse than ever predicted.

Later that morning word reached the square that several Party leaders—Zhao Ziyang, Li Peng, Qiao Shi, and Hu Qili—would visit hospitalized hunger-strikers. Zhao Shaogu, a student from the Central Academy of Fine Arts, told a reporter that visiting the students was nice, but it was still not enough. He also said that if the government did not hold substantial talks with the students, many of the hunger-strikers would take more severe measures, such as refusing to accept any kind of medical assistance, or refusing dialogue with anyone except the highest government officials.

At noon, Li Peng and other Party officials met with representatives of the hunger-striking students in the Great Hall of the People, but no decisions were reached.

Strike headquarters.

Patrick Zachmann (Magnum)

Martial law begins. A soldier declares himself sympathetic to the students' cause.

Patrick Zachmann (Magnum)

Back to Tiananmen Square—the protesters were still there, marching and shouting slogans. They seemed to be totally oblivious to the rain. Today, there are about one million people present, all showing support for the students. The people are still demonstrating, and the students are still fasting, as the sound of ambulances continues to fill the streets.

A poll conducted in the *Beijing Youth Newspaper*, May 18, 1989

On May 17, when nearly a million Beijing citizens hit the streets to show support for the hunger-strikers, our newspaper immediately organized a group to conduct a survey. Between 11:00 P.M. and midnight, we distributed 500 questionnaires to people in the square. Respondents included workers, officials, intellectuals, and private-business people. Based on the responses of the 423 returned questionnaires, the majority (over 90 percent) felt that this was a patriotic movement. Over 80 percent felt that the movement would compel the govern-

ment to give in and initiate a democracy. Below are some of the questions and responses of the survey:*

1. What do you feel this student movement is?
   a. A patriotic movement (387)
   b. Students making trouble (3)
   c. Turmoil (0)
   d. Don't know (0)
2. How do you feel about the hunger-strikers?
   a. Support them (277)
   b. Understand them (193)
   c. Don't understand them (17)
   d. Don't care (0)
3. During this movement, did you:
   a. Participate in the demonstrations (262)
   b. Donate money (240)
   c. Applaud or silently support the students (240)
   d. Not participate (5)

* Note: Respondents were allowed to choose more than one answer, which explains why the totals of the answers to questions three and four are more than 423.

4. *Who do you feel should talk to the students?*
   a. Deng Xiaoping (241)
   b. Zhao Ziyang (248)
   c. Li Peng (257)
5. *What will be the outcome of this hunger strike?*
   a. The government will meet the students' demands (280)
   b. Both sides will compromise (48)
   c. The government will suppress this movement (7)
   d. There will be great national turmoil (11)
   e. Don't know (46)

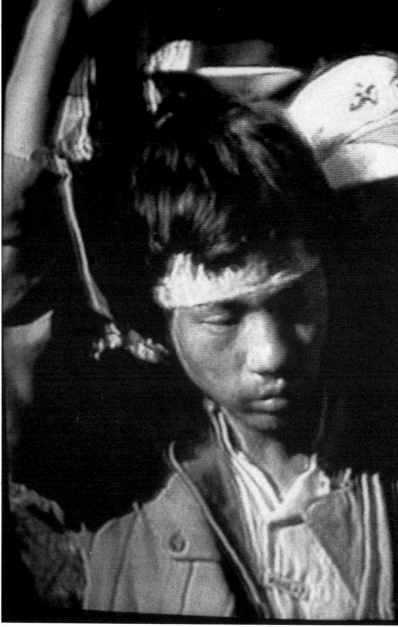

Zhao Ziyang appears with a student leader on television to persuade the strikers to stop fasting.

Superficially these hunger-strikers were "volunteers," but actually they were manipulated by some bad people. Under the circumstances, some students felt compelled to succumb to peer pressure but later regretted their decision. They were confused by the so-called support. They wanted to stop but couldn't. Of course, if you had told them that they had been taken hostage by someone, they would be unable to accept it. That's understandable.

It was quite clear from the words of student "ringleader" Wang Dan. He said, "We're choosing May 13 to stage a hunger strike in order to use the occasion of Gorbachev's visit to pressure them."

The "them," here, is our Party and government. The ringleaders' goal was to use the lives of many students as a bargaining chip—to harm the international reputation of China and the Chinese Communist Party, to blackmail the authorities, and to enlist support from international organizations. The students even expelled Red Cross rescue personnel from the scene. They set up a student patrol that would not permit endangered hunger-strikers to stop their fast and leave the square.

— *Yuan Mu, official spokesman for State Council*

The students had only two simple requests, but nobody came out to discuss them. On May 17 and May 18, only one authority was in the capital. It was not the Party Central Committee, it was not the government, it was not even the Autonomous Student Union. It was the hunger-strikers at the square. They were the supreme authority, at least in Beijing. Whatever they said, the people would comply with, and that was very important.

It was under these circumstances that the indignation of the Chinese people reached its climax. They were very angry at Deng Xiaoping because he didn't come out to speak. On the afternoon of the sixteenth, some people began to shout "Down with Deng Xiaoping!"

That evening, I started to draft the May 17 declaration. I had heard a speech of Zhao Ziyang's and I thought what he had said should be put in writing. We also decided to describe the concrete reasons why Deng Xiaoping was a dictator and should be overthrown. The declaration, however, didn't use Deng's name. On the morning of May 17 we held a meeting in the office of the Chinese Academy of Social Science, and I asked everyone to sign the declaration. Someone said that it was okay to shout "Down with Deng Xiaoping!" in the street, but it was dangerous to put it in writing. At that moment, Bao Zunxin came and said, "All right, I'll sign." He took the declaration to the square, read it to the people there, and asked them to sign it. The declaration was very favorably received. So the May 17 declaration was broadcast and it was sent to several newspapers, including one in Hong Kong. The demonstration on May 17 was the biggest ever, and Deng's reputation fell to its lowest level.

On May 18 and May 19, there was talk of storming the leader's quarters, just like the Bastille. I know for sure that some people wanted to cut off the electricity and water sup-

Zong Hoi Yi (VU)

Great Hall of the People. Upon entering, I saw nearly a company of fully armed soldiers guarding the meeting room. I just greeted the soldiers and walked right in. I also wanted to slight Li Peng, so I didn't stand up until he was in front of me. He stretched out his hand, and then I offered mine. Before he turned around, I had already sat down. My anger only increased at the sight of the man. Since April 22, we had been pleading for a meeting with Li Peng, and it was not until May 22, exactly one month later, that a meeting was allowed.

Li Peng told us that he had come "a little late." I interrupted him, and said, "Not a little late, but *much* too late." He knew this was true and didn't reply. I was really very upset, thinking that for too long China's leaders have continued to behave as emperors who could lord over us. Chinese sometimes say, "To be met by the premier is the happiest moment in one's life." It is so difficult for the Chinese to give up their habit of thanking the "emperor" for his noblesse oblige. I didn't feel thankful to Li Peng. I felt that our respect for him should depend on his abilities, not on his official title.

People throughout the country were still able to see for themselves how a twenty-one-year-old man spoke as an equal, and spoke critically no less, to the premier of the nation. We had the guts to do so because we had the truth on our side. People liked what we said because in it they heard an expression of their own anger at the government. If Zhao Ziyang had been there, I would have said the same thing. If Deng Xiaoping had come, we would have been even harsher in our criticism.

At the end of the meeting, I told Li, "You are not sincere at all. The government obviously does not want to talk to us either. Therefore, there is no point in our sitting here anymore." My heart suddenly began to race. I fell back onto the sofa and tried to grab the oxygen bag, but I couldn't reach it. I didn't lose consciousness; I just felt faint and extremely weak. Then Wang Dan said, "Kaixi, let's go." So I said, "Carry me out of here." A stretcher came and carried me out, and I was immediately rushed to the hospital.

—*Wuer Kaixi*

ply. It would be extremely dangerous and could bring about serious consequences. I was not in favor of this kind of action. There was no storming of Zhongnanhai because the student movement advocated nonviolence, reason, and peace. It should be left to future generations to judge whether what the students advocated was right or wrong.

—*Yan Jiaqi*

Right after I left the hospital, Wang Chaohua said to me: "Kaixi, let's go and meet Li Peng."

"Let's go," I replied.

I don't know exactly how she managed to arrange this meeting. Ironically, it was held in the Xinjiang Room* of the

---

* Wuer Kaixi is not ethnic Chinese. His family is from Xinjiang, an autonomous region in northwest China.

M

ARTIAL LAW

inner at the Beijing Hotel had been going well on the night of May 19, but was promptly spoiled as the news went around that Li Peng was about to make an "important speech" on television. I made my way to a friend's room on an upper level of the hotel to watch. Li Peng, looking like a scoutmaster, shoulders hunched and eyes blank, was addressing a massed audience of Party and military elders who seemed miffed at having been roused from their beds at such an unearthly hour. The situation in the capital has deteriorated drastically, Li was saying. It had become imperative to bring in units of the PLA to restore order. The whole Party and people are united as one in supporting this firm and decisive move by the Party center, and so forth. I decided to return to the square to join the reception party for the incoming troops.

The mood at the Monument in the early morning hours of May 20 was somber. The Western television crews had their cameras focused on the east and west entries from Changan Avenue. Students were bedded down all around but few were sleeping. The whole square seemed to be listening, straining to catch the distant sounds of the approaching army.

I became aware of a figure sitting in the shadows by the ballustrade. "What college are you from?" I asked. "I'm not a student," he replied, smiling rather uneasily. "How about you?" "I'm a researcher," I said. It seemed that neither of us wished to elaborate. I felt sure that I was the first foreigner he had ever talked to. Clearly, he had studiously pored over

Reading pamphlets,
downtown Beijing.
Patrick Zachmann (Magnum)

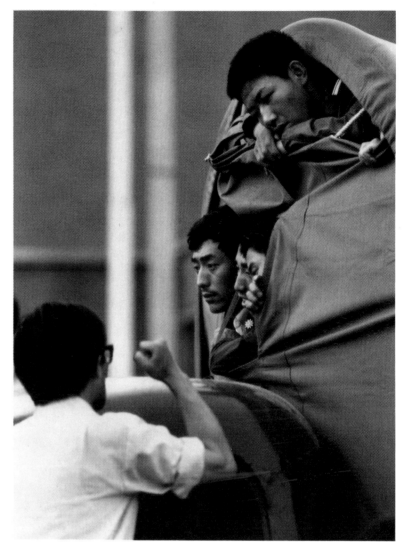

A civilian lectures members of the PLA.   *Jacques Langevin (Sygma)*

his English primers and now seemed almost desperate in his need to try them out. The effect was excruciating.

Just then, my mounting annoyance was forestalled as he smiled and said, "Do you know who I am?"

I said, "Who are you?"

"I'm a military officer," he beamed. "But please don't tell anyone here, will you?"

He said his unit was based in Shaanxi Province and that he was on leave in Beijing visiting relatives. More likely, I thought, he was an agent sent by the PLA command, and his job was to gauge the amount of opposition the troops could expect when they arrived to clear the square. But then, he seemed a rather unlikely candidate for such a mission. Perhaps he was just a very bad spy.

We discussed the impending arrival of the PLA, his face lighting up with a look of deep professional pride. He related the various routes the troops would be taking into the capital, the types of trucks they would be using, how fast they would be traveling, and, therefore (checking his watch), their estimated time of arrival. This was certainly instructive, but it only enhanced my growing sense of how surreal the situation was.

He clearly sympathized with the students—that was

A troop convoy on its way to central Beijing
meets with resistance.
Peter Turnley (Black Star)

A PLA soldier.   *Kenneth Jarecke (Contact Press Images)*

why he had come: he wanted to be a witness and participant in their historic struggle, to stand on the students' side of the barricades, and to this extent he was there as an ordinary Chinese citizen. But the soldier in him regarded the young students all around us with an almost haughty eye.

"These students are very naive, you know," he said. "They think that the troops won't open fire on them if ordered to do so. They're quite wrong. The PLA is highly disciplined; the soldiers cannot disobey orders, and they'll do whatever they're told to do. The army is on its way now and nothing can stop it."

Nimbly switching modes, he then proceeded to launch into an elaborate bilingual account of the geographical distribution of the tomato. "It's a funny thing, you know, but in Chinese we have two different words for the tomato: *fanqie* and *xihongshi*. And the tomato is not even indigenous to China! The fact is, the tomato comes from Brazil—or perhaps it's Iraq? Anyway, how is one to explain the Chinese language having two different terms for this vegetable?" Tilting his head and spreading his palms in a gesture of wonderment, he fixed me with a look of challenging, quizzical intensity. I confessed that I, too, was mystified by the thing—and at the same time made a mental note to abandon all expecta-

The students use pro-demonstration issues of
The Liberation Daily to promote their cause.
Greg Girard (Impact)

Demonstrations, petitioning, class boycotts (and) strikes are prohibited. . . . Citizens are forbidden to create rumors by any means. . .

tions of normality for the rest of the night.

All had been quiet in the square for several hours, when suddenly, around 3:30 A.M., the student loudspeakers burst back to life. "Students! The people of Beijing have stopped the advance of the People's Liberation Army at the Hujialou intersection!" A few seconds elapsed as the true impact of this momentous news began to dawn on the exhausted students in the square, and then a joyous roar of triumph went up all around.

Amazed, I turned toward my companion, but he was looking puzzled and more than a little skeptical. "It's not possible, don't believe it," he said. "The students are just spreading rumors now." Less than half an hour later, a second announcement was made from the command center on the Monument: "The people of Beijing have blocked the army in the west, at Wukesong!" Then, minutes later, the same thing was announced as having happened at Fengtai and Liuliqiao in the southwest of the city, and at Donggaodi

in the south, and so on, until eventually it was announced that the army's advance had been halted at all major points of entry into the capital. Probably two million Chinese had taken to the streets of Beijing, determined to protect the students at all costs.

My officer friend, however, was not yet convinced. Looking at his watch, he was still deep in his own calculations—numbers of troops, types of transport trucks, road speeds, distances, times, and so on. Suddenly he looked up, frowned and said, "They should have been here by now. Damn it, perhaps it's true!" Then he grinned broadly.

—*Robin Munro, a senior research associate for Asia Watch in New York City*

I arrived at the square at 9:25 A.M. on May 20. The students had stopped fasting the night before, and here and there I saw buckets of steaming rice porridge. That was the

The night of May 25.

Patrick Zachmann (Magnum)

Some students have such a poor understanding of democracy. On the day I suggested the hunger strike, I knew in the back of my mind that it would be futile.

only thing doctors said the hunger-strikers could eat.

At ten o'clock sharp, hundreds of loudspeakers began to blare out the martial law regulations:

> During the period of martial law, demonstrations, petitioning, class boycotts, strikes, any activities that will upset the city's normal routine, are prohibited. . . . Citizens are forbidden to create and/or spread rumors by any means: networking, public speeches, leaflets, and instigating social turmoil. . . . Furthermore, armed police and PLA soldiers have the right to exercise any force necessary to stop or prevent any violation of martial law orders.

But huge crowds continued to gather at the square.

During the government announcement, five helicopters appeared from the west, over Changan Avenue. At first, people thought they had been sent by airline employees to support the students. Everyone cheered and applauded. But as they got closer, the green military camouflage became visible. "Get out!" people shouted, waving their fists at the helicopters. The choppers circled around the square and headed back west. Everyone grew nervous.

Fifteen minutes later, the helicopters returned. This time they were much lower. They tilted inward to circle the square, and I could see the pilots.

Around the monument, the student broadcast system announced: "According to reliable sources, Li Peng, Yang Shangkun and Bo Yibo have staged a coup. They have formed an illegitimate government and now control part of the army. They have become our enemies. General Secretary Zhao Ziyang is under house arrest. Fellow students, the crucial moment has come. Let's unite and overthrow the illegitimate government of Li Peng. Down with the illegitimate Fascist government!"

Rumors mixed with facts kept pouring out of the loud-

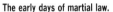
The early days of martial law.   *Alon Reininger (Contact Press Images)*

May 23. Mao's portrait is splattered with paint . . .

Shunsuke Akatsuka (Reuters-Bettmann Archive)

CHILDREN OF THE DRAGON

The portrait is removed . . .   *Erica Lansner (Black Star)*

And a new one is hung in its place.   *Garrige Ho (Reuters-Bettmann Archive)*

speakers. One rumor said that seven ministries, including the Foreign Ministry had formally denounced the Li Peng government. Another claimed that the Shanghai government had seceded, and still another that Zhao still controlled the Beijing Military Region, the *People's Daily,* and CCTV.

At the northwest corner of the square I ran into a man in his forties. He was wearing civilian clothes, but he had a button on his chest that identified him as an airman. He said he had been sent to give coordinates to the choppers. "Watch out," he said. "They'll soon drop tear gas canisters from the helicopters. I can't say anything more, but my heart is on your side."

At noon, the student loudspeakers began advising people on how to protect themselves from tear gas. "Stay low and use wet towels to cover your eyes, nose, and mouth." Instantly, long lines appeared in front of the water fountains.

A few minutes later, the same announcer said, "Attention! Attention! Important correction: They will use a different type of gas, everyone must use not a damp towel, but a dry one to cover his or her mouth." She repeated the message again and again.

The helicopters hovered overhead. I faced west, from which the troops were supposed to be coming. I took a deep breath, trying to sniff any trace of tear gas, but I didn't smell anything. All my senses were heightened. I was ready to flee at any second.

Around 1:00 P.M., in the middle of another student broadcast, a female voice suddenly cut in, "I just came back from Liuliqiao. . . ." She paused to catch her breath. "Armed police have beaten us with clubs . . . they pointed guns at us . . . fifty-four people were injured. There is blood all over my shirt. We desperately need reinforcements at Liuliqiao!"

Soon, truckloads of young people shouting and waving school banners rushed westward. I followed them on my bike. As I left, I heard a male voice from the student loudspeakers telling the crowds to use wet towels after all to protect themselves when the tear gas came.

Around 11:00 P.M., a female voice calmly announced over the PA system: "Any student who can find kites, please try to fly them over the square. They can prevent the helicopters from hovering above us." I looked up and saw two tiny kites drifting up and down against the dark night sky.

The broadcast stopped. It was quiet. Rumors abounded. Someone said that a division had gathered in a secret tunnel (under) the Great Hall of the People.

All the students sat packed tightly together in the square. The government broadcast had stopped and it was quiet. Rumors abounded. The most frightening one said that the subway, which had been sealed off during the day, was going be used to transport troops. There were four subway entrances on the south side of the square. In addition, someone said that more than a division had gathered in a secret tunnel that connected the Great Hall of the People and the Communist party leadership compound at Zhongnanhai. They could rush out any minute to assault the square.

Tens of thousands of onlookers were gathered in small groups, standing around, talking quietly with one another. Some sprawled over on the broad steps in front of the Great Hall of the People. I took a photograph of them, and as the flash went off, a woman grabbed me.

"Why are you taking my picture?" She questioned me and demanded to see my ID. When I gave it to her, she became friendly. "I'm a reporter too," she said. "I'm so worried about these kids, but I don't know what good I can do. I just feel I have to be here with them tonight." She kept on shaking her head, and murmured to herself, "They ought to get out of the square. It is getting too dangerous, too dangerous."

—*Peng Ling, a graduate student from China*

Chai Ling is a very ordinary young woman. She is attractive but not a stunning beauty. She is smart but not a political genius. She is charming, but she does not have an endless font of charisma. What makes her so beautiful, brilliant, and beguiling is that she so perfectly represents her peers. She embodies the ordinary, straightforward, no-nonsense dreams of those in China struggling to realize their dreams of freedom, democracy, and a better life. Chai Ling was willing to step forward and take the initiative when it was necessary.

From left to right: Chai Ling, Wuer Kaixi, Wang Dan, and a translator.

Zong Hoi Yi (VU)

A plainclothes cop said that the sentence for counterrevolutionary activities is seventeen (years). I'd be forty after seventeen years in prison.

On the morning of May 28, 1989, Chai Ling, flustered, frightened, and crying, came looking for me at the Beijing Hotel. Tiananmen was still occupied by student forces but spirits were flagging. The students were now beginning to fight among themselves. The main rift was between the fresh recruits from the provinces, who were looking for action, and the tired students from Beijing, who were trying to maintain control and somehow be democratic at the same time. The student leaders were responsible for the welfare of tens of thousands of followers; millions more watched their every move to see where the nation was headed.

Chai Ling found me with the help of a young man I shall call Wang Li. Wang was an activist from Xian who was living on the square when I met him. He was one of several students whom the BBC interviewed or who offered us help in one form or another. In return, I let him use my room to telephone, shower, and rest. Wang Li brought Chai Ling to the Western Dining Room, where I was having Sunday breakfast with a friend.

She looked tired, dusty, wounded, and angry. One sensed that she could explode at any minute. She smiled nervously at me and asked, "Can you help me?" I said yes. All I could fathom from bits of guarded conversation at breakfast was that some kind of threat had been made against her, she wanted to talk, and she was going to run away.

She started out by saying, "These may be my last words. My name is Chai Ling. I am twenty-three years old . . ." but soon she was crying. I stopped the interview while she cried, but she wiped away her tears and insisted that we continue. Once she got going, the words came in a torrent. I felt questions would have been an intrusion, breaking the rhythm of her story, so I just let her go on and on. We listened in rapt silence. Chai Ling was racked with pain, disappointment, and guilt.

She despaired that all would be lost if the students

Once martial law had been declared, the movement's momentum slipped.   *Zong Hoi Yi (VU)*

ended up fighting among themselves; she told me that some had already sold out to the government. She didn't know who to trust anymore. I think the possibility that the movement would be destroyed from within scared her more than the armed troops who were slowly closing in on the city.

Only two weeks before, hundreds had followed her lead and pledged themselves to refuse all food until the government recognized their demands. Today she was fleeing. What would her friends and followers think of her? What about those left in the square? The responsibility was frightening. But what haunted her more was, given the unwritten pact of love and trust between leader and followers, how could she not remain with them to the end?

Chai Ling asked if we could swing by Tiananmen one last time before leaving. She wanted to see if Feng Congde would leave with her now. All we knew was that he was somewhere in the square. We found Feng but lost Chai Ling in the crowd. We assumed that she had fled to the train station. But at around 5:00 P.M. my phone rang. It was Chai Ling. She said she wanted to visit Beida one last time to see her friends. Later that same evening she decided not to flee

Changan Avenue.   *Alon Reininger (Contact Press Images)*

Students at the Central Academy of Fine Arts
shape the Goddess of Democracy.
Erica Lansner (Black Star)

Detachments of the PLA arrive on the square.

Dario Mitidieri (Select)

after all. I think what convinced her to stay till the end was the warm welcome at Beida and her election as commander in chief of the movement. If she were powerless to influence events, I think she would have been able to walk away. Instead she was appointed top leader and now, given her determination to live up to her friends' expectations of her, she simply could not leave.

—Phillip Cunningham, a graduate student of Chinese history at the University of Michigan

I think these may be my last words. My name is Chai Ling. I am twenty-three years old. My home is in Shandong Province. I entered Beijing University in 1983 and majored in psychology. I began my graduate studies at Beijing Normal University in 1987. By coincidence, my birthday is April 15, the day Hu Yaobang died. . . .

The situation has become so dangerous. The students asked me what we were going to do next. I wanted to tell them that we were expecting bloodshed, that it would take a massacre, which would spill blood like a river through Tiananmen Square, to awaken the people. But how could I tell them this? How could I tell them that their lives would have to be sacrificed in order to win?

If we withdraw from the square, the government will kill us anyway and purge those who supported us. If we let them win, thousands would perish, and seventy years of achievement would be wasted. Who knows how long it would be before the movement could rise again? The government has so many means of repression—execution, isolation. They can wear you down and that's exactly what they did to Wei Jingsheng.

I love those kids out there so much. But I feel so helpless. How can I change the world? I am only one person. I never wanted any power. But my conscience will not permit me to surrender my power to traitors and schemers. I want to scream at Chinese people everywhere that we are so miserable! We should not kill each other anymore! Our chances are too slim as it is.

I was extremely sad because, once again, I saw all kinds of people trying to betray us and put an end to this movement. At the start of the hunger strike there were about a thousand students participating, ruining their health. It infuriates me to think that there are people who want to ruin

A PLA soldier.
Jacques Langevin (Sygma)

Making an appeal to the occupying soldiers.

Patrick Zachmann (Magnum)

what these 1,000—and later several thousand—students are risking their lives for.

Within the intellectual circle, however, two supportive friends suggested that we call things off and take on another duty, like writing a book to be entitled *Let the Whole World Know*. They also said that if this book were circulated, the world would be told exactly what was going on. Then we could be satisfied at the sight of our execution.

I had a conversation with a plainclothes cop on April 25. I asked him what the sentence was for counterrevolutionary activities. He said that it used to be three to five years, but now it is seventeen. I'd be forty after seventeen years in prison. I'm really not willing to do that.

Yesterday I told my husband that I was no longer willing to stay in China. I realize that many students won't understand why I'm withdrawing from this movement and I will probably be criticized for this. But I hope that while I can no longer continue with this work there will be others who can. Democracy isn't the result of just one person's efforts. During the hunger strike I had said that we were not fighting so that we could die but so that we could live. I was fighting for life, because democracy cannot be accomplished

by a single generation. Now I'm even more convinced of this. If I don't die, I vow to teach my child, from the day he is born, to grow up to be an honest, kind, fair, and independent Chinese.

We were striving for rights, and I felt like telling everyone, including undercover police and soldiers, that the rights that the students were risking their lives for were also for them. I would be ashamed to enjoy the benefits of these rights we are struggling for if I had never participated in this movement.

I have felt depressed many times. Some of the students have such a poor understanding of democracy. On the day that I suggested the hunger strike, I knew in the back of my mind that it would be futile. There are certain people and certain events in history that are destined to fail. In spite of all this, I have always tried to come across as a strong role model for the students and let them know that some day we will win.

I believe that democracy is a natural desire. It should guarantee human rights and independence, and foster self-respect—all of which people are entitled to.

Unfortunately, the basic human instinct for indepen-

During the evening, martial law.
Zong Hoi Yi (VU)

Around 3:30 A.M. the student loudspeakers burst back to life. "Students! The people of Beijing have stopped the army's advance at the Hujialou intersection!"

dence has been greatly inhibited and degraded among the Chinese. Some out-of-town students even came to us, asking for food, lodging, and instructions for what to do next. I thought, they have hands, eyes, their own minds; they can take care of themselves. They are supporting a very good cause but, honestly, many of these students are irresponsible; they are accustomed to living in a feudal society in which they do not have to make decisions for themselves.

The square is our last stand. If we lose it, China will retreat into another dark age, the people will once again turn against one other, with no real feelings or communication between them. If a nation's own people don't stay and help it to grow and develop, who will? But I will not be there to protect the square because I'm different from the others: my name is on the blacklist. I don't want to die.

Before this movement, I dreamt about going abroad—to study psychology—but friends warned me not to think of America as a paradise. They said that there are a lot of overseas Chinese there and that their competitive

instincts were overwhelming. I want to say to all those Chinese outside of China, those who already have freedom and democracy, and who have never had their lives endangered, to stand up and unite, to put an end to the fighting among us. There are so many kids here risking their own lives for what you have. Do what you can, break down the barriers and don't be selfish anymore. Think about our race. One billion people can't just fade away.

—*Chai Ling*

At 8:00 P.M., I came out of my tent to find a few students shouting at the officers and soldiers near our station. I walked over to listen. Excitedly, they told the soldiers, "The students are patriotic. Why are the troops coming to control them?" "Didn't you see all the people coming out to support the students? Some of your troops even showed their sympathy with them. Don't listen to what the government has said." Their words were poisonous, bewitching, and in-

"These students are very naive, you know. . . . The PLA is highly disciplined; the soldiers cannot disobey orders and they'll do whatever they're told to do."

citing. Some soldiers remained silent; others walked away.

I returned to my tent, the voices of these self-righteous students still echoing in my ears. Between the orders and decisions coming from the Party Central Committee and the abuse hurled by these people, how can the soldiers think clearly?

And how can the students say this is a "patriotic" movement while at the same time purposely sabotaging the worldwide attention generated by the Sino-Soviet summit, which is also "patriotic?" Our soldiers must not be intimidated by these lies.

At a time like this, I thought to myself, the most important thing is to keep my head clear as an army political cadre. First, I must withstand the test of this political tempest; at the same time, I must instruct the troops to neither listen to nor believe the lies. I will never let even one soldier become a "political captive" of these students.

In order to keep the minds of our officers and soldiers politically alert, in order to meet this political struggle, I drafted three ways to deal with the situation:

1. Let the military scouts returning from Tiananmen Square share their feelings on whether they think this is a riot.

2. Study the Party Central Committee's instructions once again to make the whole battalion realize the social background and sinister political motives behind this riot.

3. Let all the cadres and soldiers keep an eye on each other, consciously guarding against listening to or believing rumors; never become a "political captive"!

—Shi Renquan, an officer in the People's Liberation Army; a member of the martial law troops that occupied Beijing

On Thursday, May 25, around 5:30 P.M., I got a call at home from Professor Li Shuxian, wife of Professor Fang Lizhi. She asked me to come to their apartment in a car as soon as possible. She and her son, Fang Zhe, were at home; Professor Fang had left the day before for a professional conference in Taiyuan. Professor Li was very frightened. She was convinced that the arrest of their family was imminent and wanted to leave immediately. She asked if I would bring her and her son to the railroad station, and I agreed. She wore a big straw hat and was careful to say nothing that might indicate to the taxi driver who she was. At the railroad station, her son stayed to see her off but told me he would not leave Beijing. Professor Li did not tell me her destination, except to say that she was going to be with Professor Fang at a "pre-agreed-upon" location.

The next afternoon, again around 5:00 P.M., a close friend of the Fang family called me and asked if he could see me. When the friend arrived, he told me the Fangs were in Taiyuan, but that they had already been recognized and that hiding was impossible. After a while he very tentatively asked me if, should there be no other recourse, I thought the Fangs could go to the U.S. embassy for protection. I said I would try to find an answer.

Two days later, at a dinner party on May 27, I saw an embassy official. The party was full of American journalists, so I had to ask the question very quietly and quickly. The answer I got was also very brief: such things are highly awkward and complicated and could lead to de facto imprisonment for the persons concerned. Nevertheless, the official said he would broach the matter, however tentatively, next time there was an appropriate occasion to do so inside the embassy.

Professors Fang and Li returned to Beijing the evening of Sunday, May 28, and invited my family and me to see them in the late afternoon of May 29. They said they had been constantly tailed by the police in Taiyuan. Professor Li was especially upset, indeed was almost unable to control her anger and fear. I repeated what the official had told me, and they replied that they were not considering asking any embassy for help at that point, dangerous though the situation might be.

—Perry Link, a professor of Chinese literature at Princeton University

Nothing excites a sculptor as much as seeing a work of her own creation take shape. But although I was watching the creation of a sculpture that I had had no part in making, I nevertheless felt the same excitement. It was the "Goddess of Democracy" statue that stood for five days in Tiananmen Square.

Until last year I was a graduate student at the Central Academy of Fine Arts in Beijing, where the sculpture was made. I was living there when these events took place.

Students and faculty of the Central Academy of Fine Arts, which is located only a short distance from Tiananmen Square, had from the beginning been actively involved in the demonstrations. When the movement wanted to honor the recently deceased Hu Yaobang, the students painted a huge oil portrait of him and propped it against the Monument to the People's Heroes in the square. On May 27, a representative of the Beijing Autonomous Student Union came to the Central Academy to ask them to produce another large-scale work of art, this time a statue, and that it be completed in time for the great demonstration planned for the thirtieth. The Student Union, which gave 8,000 yuan for materials and

A woman lodges a plea with soldiers in a halted troop carrier.
David C. Turnley (Black Star)

expenses, suggested that the sculpture be a replica of the Statue of Liberty, like the one that had been carried by demonstrators in Shanghai two days earlier. But the Central Academy sculpture students rejected that idea, both because it might be taken as too openly pro-American and because copying an existing work was contrary to their principles as creative artists. What was needed, they felt, was a new, specifically Chinese symbol. But they faced a problem: how could an original, major sculpture be finished in three days, even if they worked through the nights?

Their solution was ingenious, and explains some features of the sculpture as it took shape: its slightly off-balance look and its posture with two hands raised to hold up its torch. The students, with the strong academic training that young artists receive in China, chose a thoroughly academic approach to their problem: they decided to adapt to their purpose a studio practice work that one of them had already made, a foot-and-a-half-high clay sculpture of a nude man grasping a pole with two raised hands and leaning his weight on it. It had been done originally as a demonstration of how the musculature and distribution of weight are affected when the center of gravity is shifted outside the body. This was the unlikely beginning from which the Goddess of Liberty and Democracy was to grow. The students cut off the lower part of the pole and added a flame at the top to turn it into a torch; they repositioned the body into a more upright position; they changed the man's face to that of a woman, added breasts, and finally draped the whole figure in a robe.

This transformed model was the basis for the thirty-seven-foot-high statue. It was first cut into four horizontal sections, and teams of young sculptors constructed the corresponding parts of the huge work, which would be assembled on the square. The main material was foam plastic, large pieces of it carved and held together by wire, with plaster added to the surface to join the pieces more strongly and to allow finer modeling. The four sections were fairly light, each needing only five or six students to lift.

The students had intended to bring the statue in in one of the academy's trucks. But the Security Bureau sent word that any driver daring to take them would lose his license. In the end, the students hired six Beijing carts, a bicycle in front and a flat cart with two wheels behind; four of these carried the sections of the statue, the other two carried the tools and materials.

The route had been announced: turn left out of the academy, then westward to the Donghuamen, the east gate of the Forbidden City, around the road between the wall and the moat to the square. Our announcement was made to deceive the police, in case they were waiting to stop us. In fact, we turned right out of the academy and followed the shorter route, down Wangfujing, right along Changan Avenue, past the Beijing Hotel.

The site on the square where the statue was to be erected had been carefully chosen. It was on a great axis, heavy with

Protection from tear gas.
Gabriel (VU)

The statue was made so that once assembled it could not be taken apart again, but would have to be destroyed all at once.

both cosmological and political symbolism, extending from the main entrance of the Forbidden City, with the huge portrait of Mao Zedong over it; through the Monument to the People's Heroes, which had become the command headquarters of the student movement. The statue was to be set up just across Changan Avenue from Mao so that it would confront him face-to-face. When we arrived around 10:30 at night, a huge crowd, perhaps 50,000 people, had gathered around the tall scaffolding of iron poles that had already been erected to support the statue. The parts were placed one on another, attached to this iron frame; plaster was poured into the hollow core, vertical poles extended from the ground up through the center to hold it upright. The exposed iron supports were then cut away, leaving the statue freestanding. It stood on a base also made of rods, about six feet in height, which was later covered with cloth. The statue was made so that once assembled it could not be taken apart again but would have to be destroyed all at once.

The work continued through the night. A circle of students joined hands around the statue so that those working on it would be undisturbed. By noon on May 30, it was ready for the unveiling ceremony, for which many people had waited all night. Actually, only the face was "veiled" by two pieces of cloth, bright blue and red—the students never collected enough cloth to cover the whole figure.

The ceremony was simple and very moving. A statement had been prepared about the meaning of the statue and was read by a woman, probably a student at the Broadcasting Academy, who had a good Mandarin accent. "We have made this statue," the statement said, "as a memorial to democracy, and to express our respect for the hunger-strikers, for the students who have stayed in the square so many days, and for all others involved in the movement." Two Beijing residents, a woman and a man, had been chosen at random from the crowd and invited into the circle to pull the strings that would "unveil" the sculpture. When the cloths

May 30. The Goddess of Democracy makes her appearance on the square.   *Zong Hoi Yi (VU)*

Brought to the square on the backs of three
bicycle carts, the statue receives some final touches.
Alon Reininger (Contact Press Images)

fell, the crowd burst into cheers, there were shouts of "Long live democracy!" and other slogans, and some began to sing the "Internationale." A musical performance was given by students from the Central Academy of Music: choral renditions of the "Hymn to Joy" from Beethoven's Ninth Symphony, another foreign song and one Chinese, and finally the "Internationale" again.

That night there were strong winds and rain. We rushed to the square in the morning to see if the statue had been damaged. But it had endured this first serious test without harm. We took this as a good omen. . . .

—*Cao Xinyuan, a sculptor*

Before leaving Beijing, I went to Tiananmen to say good-bye to the students, especially those from the Central Academy of Fine Arts, where I had taught before I left for the West. They asked me to say something. But what could I say? I wanted to tell them to get away from the square for their own safety, but they said they had already written their wills. If it took blood to achieve the goal, they were willing to make the sacrifice. I told them to stay calm even though the authorities might arrest and imprison them, as they had done before. Then they asked me what it was like in jail. They were very young. I knew that they had no idea of what jail was like under the Communist regime. I didn't tell them my own experience during the Cultural Revolution. Instead, I told them that people would remember them forever for what they had done, and that jail was not that horrible. I quoted Gorky: "Jail and hospitals are the best schools." Upon hearing this, they all came up to me and asked me to write these words on their shirts. I thought I could give them moral support and comfort by doing this. As I wrote, tears rolled down my face.

—*Zhang Langlang, a writer*

The Goddess of Democracy.

The June 2 Hunger Strike Declaration

We protest! We appeal! We repent! We are on hunger strike. What we seek is not death but a true life. Chinese intellectuals must rid themselves of spineless political behavior; they speak out but never act. We now call for the birth of a new political culture!

Our hunger strike is no longer a petition but a protest against martial law. We advocate democratization in China through peaceful means; we oppose all forms of violence. However, we do not fear violent suppression. The imposition of martial law has brought shame to the Communist party, the government, and the army; it has ruined the accomplishments of ten years of reform in one stroke.

China's entire history has been shaped by political violence. Since 1949, slogans such as "taking class struggle as the key link" have pushed to its extremity our traditional psychology of hate and the vicious age-old cycle of violence.

Martial law epitomizes the political culture of class struggle. But hatred can only produce violence and dictatorship. We must build Chinese democracy on a foundation of tolerance and cooperation. Democratic politics is politics without enemies, without hatred. It is a politics of respect, tolerance, compromise, and the electoral process. Prime Minister Li Peng has made major errors and should resign according to democratic procedures—but Li Peng is not our enemy. Even if he steps down he should still be permitted to enjoy the rights of every citizen, including the right to his own ideas.

This student movement has won unprecedented sympathy and support from the whole of society. Up to now, our supporters have lacked a sense of themselves as citizens. They must now begin to try to understand the concept of equal rights—every citizen's rights are equal to those of even the prime minister.

But the government has ignored the basic rights endowed upon every citizen by the constitution and has declared this movement to be a form of turmoil. This stems from their dictatorial notion of politics, and it has bred a series of mistaken decisions and confrontation. Therefore the real agent of turmoil is the government itself. It has been due to the self-restraint of the demonstrators that massive bloodshed has been avoided. The government must admit its mistakes. We do not think a correction now would be too late.

The true realization of democracy lies in the democratization of governmental procedures, in its methods and operation. So we appeal to the Chinese people: get rid of the tradition of pure ideology making and sloganeering! This is empty rhetoric. It is time to begin turning our talk into democratic practice.

It must be admitted that the idea of democratic government is strange to every Chinese. We must learn from the very beginning—all of us, including the top leaders of the Party and state. In the process, mistakes by the government and by the people will be inevitable. The key lies in acknowledging our mistakes and in correcting them when they occur. By learning from our mistakes we will learn to govern our country democratically.

Citizens' consciousness is not just a sense of justice and sympathy. Everyone must become an active participant in the building of democracy, for civic consciousness is also a matter of shared responsibility and obligations. Everybody is first and foremost a citizen and only second a student, a professor, a cadre, a soldier, or even premier.

The removal of one unpopular leader and the entry of another cannot reach the roots of the problem. We need not a savior but a democratic system. So we appeal to society to establish an independent political force as a check to government decision making. The essence of democracy is balance of power—better ten devils to watch each other than one saint with absolute power.

Marches, hunger strikes, and similar actions are democratic ways of expressing the popular will. They are entirely legitimate and reasonable, and in no way constitute "turmoil."

MASSACRE

On the night of June 2 we were walking down the street when we heard: "The troops have entered Beijing! Tiananmen Square has been surrounded!" Immediately, people began barricading the route with trash carts and bicycle carts. We encountered a bus without a license plate at the Xinjiekou* intersection. The bus was filled with young men, all with the same white shirts and crew cuts. They were supposed to be in disguise, but it was obvious that they were soldiers. Some were plainly apprehensive. We began shouting at them, "You soldiers don't even have the guts to wear your uniforms or show military plates!"

People were swearing and shouting, pleased with themselves for having stopped the bus. The bus tried to make a U-turn to leave, but a young man pushed his bicycle cart in front of it and shouted at the top of his lungs, "Students! Block the other side!" But the driver skillfully swerved around the bicycle cart. I asked myself, "Should I stand in front of it and block it?" We all hesitated for a moment, and then the bus was gone. The young man said angrily, "You college boys are all cowards! How can you fight for democracy?"

The next morning, Changan Avenue was packed with people. Several army buses were stopped on the road with their tires slashed. Inside them, people had found bayonets, machine guns, ammunition, and bags of butcher knives. These were displayed on top of the bus.

* Xinjiekou is the intersection of Xisi and Fuchengmen roads, northwest of Beihai Park.

Jianguomen, one of the twelve overpasses in Beijing,
is one of the main arteries to the square.
Gabriela Medina P.

The soldiers rolled up the windows and we could see them sweating inside. A young man punched at one of the windows with his fist. "Open the window!" He kept shouting. "Open up! The last time you guys came, we gave you food and water. Nobody's going to feed you this time! You know those four people on hunger strike in the square? You're going to join them!" As he was talking, he kept pounding the window. I said to him, "Please stop that. It's not all their fault." But he pushed me aside and roared at me, "You college kids! Don't be stupid! If you side with them, we won't side with you!" I didn't know what to say.

—*Yang Jianli, mathematics graduate student*

At about 5:00 P.M. on Saturday, June 3, I returned to Xinhuamen, the front entrance of the Communist party headquarters. People were gathered there, angrily talking about what had happened that afternoon. There was an old woman among them, leaning on her son, tearfully telling the soldiers: "You shouldn't use guns against students. How will you explain it to your parents?" The soldiers were only eighteen or nineteen years old. They weren't permitted to respond, but they couldn't shut out what people said either. Several soldiers burst out crying. An officer stood behind them, removing those who wept.

Around 11:00 P.M., as I walked westward away from the square I saw people on bicycles rushing toward it, shouting hysterically, "Soldiers are killing civilians!" No one could believe the killing had started.

—*Hou Tianming, a Beijing lawyer*

When we got to the square, we saw no sign of panic. By now, after all the excitement, I decided that I had lost my fear. I said to H., "This afternoon, I was still afraid of being hit by a billy club. But now I think we ought to fight with them. Let's get ourselves a pair of clubs. Tear gas and water cannons won't kill anyone. It's summer, you know." While I was going on in this vein, I heard a sharp noise from the west side of Changan Avenue. "A gunshot!" I said. Suddenly my heart was in my throat. I couldn't speak. A middle-aged woman shouted at us, "Don't go any farther! They've already started firing!"

"Let's turn back," I said to myself, but H. was saying "Hurry up!" and pedaling toward the gunfire. I forced myself to follow him.

Gradually, we saw that there were fires at the Xidan intersection. The buses that people set up yesterday as barricades were now on fire. Tanks and truckloads of soldiers armed with machine guns were rolling in one after another toward the square. At the intersection, we heard perhaps a thousand people shouting "Down with fascism!" We threw our bicycles aside and joined the crowd. We made our way to the very front and began shouting together with the rest,

Tents protect the Goddess of Democracy from government officials determined to remove it.
Atsuko Ohtsuka (Photo Shuttle: Japan)

June 3, afternoon. Students clash with police.   *Jacques Langevin (Sygma)*

"Down with fascism!" Flashes spouted from the muzzles of the soldiers' rifles. We ran back a bit and threw ourselves onto the pavement. "Did they really fire?" I said to H. "I still can't believe it." Some people continued to stand up, saying nonchalantly, "Don't be frightened, they're only using rubber bullets." Before they had finished speaking I heard someone scream, "Look out! There's a cart coming through!" Two men with gunshot wounds were being carried away. Someone swore and gasped, "They aren't rubber bullets at all!" One man had been shot in the leg; the other was hit in the stomach and died on the cart. We stood beside the cart, staring at him, and burst into tears. All this time the army trucks kept on passing in front of us in a line. As the crowd shouted "Fuck you, Deng Xiaoping, fuck you!" it pressed on toward the middle of the road. Suddenly there was more gunfire, and we dropped to the ground again; my heart jumped from sheer fright.

A voice screamed, "Get another cart!" I felt a great rage well up in me. I began gathering bricks and throwing them at the trucks. "Let's get them!" I shouted. Then the soldiers fired again, and another three or four men were carried away. H. wept and shouted, "They're dead, but we're still alive. . . . I'll fight with them to the death!" He started running forward. But I pulled him back tightly. "Don't die for nothing!" I said.

"Let's get out of here," I heard someone say from below. I looked up the street and saw twenty to thirty soldiers coming at us with fixed bayonets. Two tear-gas shells exploded, and a thick, yellowish smoke quickly spread through the crowd. I began to cough; our noses and eyes ran. My hands hurt, and I lost my voice.

Gradually the smoke cleared. An endless line of army trucks had now jammed Changan Avenue. For a moment there was complete silence. Then, little by little, the people

June 3, morning. Soldiers take up
positions on the square.
Jacques Langevin (Sygma)

We could see the soldiers sweating inside. A young man punched at one of the windows with his fist. "Open the window!" He kept shouting. "Open up!"

collected again and inched their way toward the trucks until they could touch them. They begged, they cursed, they swore. "You are the People's Army, you can't open fire on the people," some protested. Others were sarcastic, saying, "You're very good at killing unarmed civilians. You've turned yourselves into killing machines for those old bastards. But when they finally die, you'll all be executed." Then a hoarse voice began to lead the crowd in singing the "Internationale." We all wept. The soldiers were stone-faced; you could see from their eyes the stupidity, the apathy, the cruelty. The crowd grew angry again and shouted "Down with the fascists!" and "Bury Yang Shangkun's army." Some people from the back passed us bricks and stones. An officer took out a pistol and shot a young man just a few feet away, and I stood there and watched him die in front of me.

Another young man was walking alongside the army vehicles, talking to the soldiers. "Four of my best friends died in my arms today," he said, "why don't you kill me, too?" He patted his chest. "Come on, open fire," he insisted. "Open fire." Later we learned that he was a student from Xinjiang. He had walked the two miles from Muxudi* with the troops. His blue T-shirt was soaked with blood. Finally, somebody grabbed him and dragged him off the street.

"Get that officer!" someone shouted. Dozens of people had encircled a jeep. H. wanted to go up close, but I held him back. People were now pounding the jeep with their fists. There was a round of gunfire from a truck in front of us. I saw five people fall. H. dropped face down, sobbing. "I don't want to live anymore, I don't want to live."

A man came over to us, shook us, and said, "Where did you get hit?" He thought we had been wounded. His concern made us cry even harder.

Then an ambulance arrived. The doctor inside waved a Red Cross flag as the vehicle approached the soldiers, but they aimed their weapons at the ambulance and signaled it to retreat. The doctor waved the Red Cross flag even harder. More soldiers pointed their weapons at the ambulance until, finally, it began to retreat. I heard someone shout through clenched teeth, "They're not even letting people be saved now. From now on, when we see a soldier, let's kill him."

At that moment, the crowd suddenly began to shift wildly about. A mob chased two soldiers and one of them was caught.

I yelled, "Beat him to death!" and struck him. H. kicked him. The soldier cried, "It wasn't me!" When we heard this, we stopped beating him.

My heart softened, and I could tell that H. felt the same way. We turned around and walked back hand in hand, but

the two soldiers were quickly beaten to death by the civilians anyway.

—*Yang Jianli*

On the evening of June 3, a convoy was blocked and stopped by the masses at Jianguomen bridge.† One armored personnel carrier, probably that of the field commander, came to Jianguomen to issue orders of operation. It dashed around madly, crushing a number of people in its way. When it reached Jianguomen, it pushed over another military vehicle, instantly crushing a civilian to death. People chased the APC all the way to Tiananmen, where someone threw a manhole cover into its tread, breaking it. The APC started to spin around and was then set afire by the masses. When it first started to burn, those inside didn't come out for fear that they'd be attacked by the crowd. However, after it had been burning for a while, the driver, who could no longer stand the heat, emerged.

As soon as he appeared, more than a hundred people surrounded him, preparing to attack. At the time, I had two bricks in my hands and had pushed all the way to the front, ready to hit him. I was so close that I could have hit him anywhere I wanted to. In less than a couple of seconds, however, the driver was covered with blood from innumerable cuts on his face. This softened me, and I dropped the bricks. He could no longer stand upright by himself. Two people were holding him while the rest just wanted to attack. I couldn't help going up to protect him from his assailants and, in the process, received quite a beating myself. I was smeared with his blood, which made me feel nauseous. Nevertheless, it was worth defending him, because I thought it was better to let him live and catch him, than to beat him to death.

—*Liu Tang, a Beijing student*

I returned to Tiananmen Square at about 10:00 P.M. the night of June 3. From that time on, news of people being killed began to come in. I went to our broadcasting station and said on the air: "The government has now placed itself in complete opposition to the people. Li Peng has become the universal enemy of our people: he will be judged by history, and he will be nailed to history's pillar of shame. We, the Chinese people, are now called upon to sacrifice ourselves for the sake of a beautiful tomorrow." I was overexcited, and I collapsed.

I was in the last ambulance to leave Tiananmen Square. There were three wounded there with me. The man next to me was already dead. There was also an infantryman among

---

* Muxudi is the location of the military museum, west of Changan.

† Jianguomen is the location of one of Beijing's two foreign compounds.

Students searched this bus and discovered the true identity of its occupants: PLA soldiers disguised as civilians.
Alon Reininger (Contact Press Images)

"You're good at killing unarmed civilians. You've turned yourselves into killing machines for those bastards. But when they finally die, you'll all be executed."

us who had been rescued by the students. I guessed that he had probably been in the front rank and was inadvertently shot by his fellow soldiers. There was blood all over.

At the hospital I saw twenty to thirty wounded students. The doctor felt my chest to see if my heart was still beating; they had already gotten used to the routine of checking whether you were dead or alive. Students kept arriving in a steady stream with news of more deaths and of the situation in the streets.

—Wuer Kaixi

I left Beijing University at 11:30 P.M. When I reached Baishiqiao,* I sensed that something was wrong. I ran into someone going in the opposite direction. He cried as he told me, "They're killing people; many were killed around me." Others began to cry with him as they heard the news.

My first thought was, "I have to get to Tiananmen before the army does, otherwise more people will die." I knew I wouldn't be able to persuade them all to go. But I hoped that I could at least convince my Wuhan University† students to leave. I still had some influence with them.

During the movement we had talked often about dying for democracy, but that was purely hypothetical. We never dreamed we would actually have to lay down our lives; it couldn't be true. I had to see for myself.

I rode my bicycle as quickly as possible toward Muxudi. Before I arrived, I ran into someone else. Very calmly he said, "People are being killed there. Look, this is blood." Blood stains covered his clothes.

Flames lit the night sky as I got within a few hundred yards of Muxudi. Soldiers, wielding machine guns, crouched behind armored personnel carriers. I couldn't believe that this was Beijing.

---

* Baishiqiao is an area near the Beijing Library and Capital Stadium.

† Wuhan is the capital of Hubei Province.

Civilians on the square attempt to persuade soldiers to side with their cause.

Alon Reininger (Contact Press Images)

More than a hundred people surrounded him, preparing to attack. At the time, I had two bricks in my hands and had pushed all the way to the front.

I didn't know Beijing very well, but I knew that following Changan Avenue would be the easiest way to get to the square. At first I rode on the sidewalk. Then I saw that many civilians were hiding behind trees on the sidewalk and throwing stones at the soldiers who were shooting back. I decided it was safer to ride on the road, next to the soldiers. Rocks and bricks pelted the army vehicles. Many windshields were broken. From the apartment buildings along the avenue people chanted "Fascists! Dogs!"

I saw a young girl walking toward me along the sidewalk. She was weeping while murmuring to herself: "What is this all about? Why? Why?"

Then, at 12:30 A.M. on June 4, I saw the first corpse: a twenty-year-old man wearing a headband and a mask. He was lying on the concrete divider between the bicycle and automobile lanes, 200 yards from Muxudi.

I had to get off my bike at times to avoid riding over broken glass and scattered rocks. At other times I was so close to the army trucks that I could touch them. The sol-

diers were surprised to see me; I was the only civilian traveling among them. The soldiers shot at the people who were shouting and throwing rocks, but for the most part they were firing over the heads of the people. Their bullets struck nearby apartment buildings. Sometimes I felt the impulse to kneel before them, to beg them to stop. Bullets zipped over my head. I was frightened and thought about my wife and child. But I knew if I did not get to Tiananmen as soon as I could, I would not be able to live with myself.

I finally caught up with the forward troop detachment at Xidan. I was about a hundred yards from them. The soldiers stopped and waited for the APCs to clear the roadblock. I didn't dare go forward any more. Instead, I took a road that paralleled Changan Avenue. Along the way to the square, I saw about a dozen people who had been shot.

It was around 1:00 A.M. when I got to the square. The atmosphere was weirdly calm, almost lazy in fact. I found the people from the Workers' Federation and told them with tears in my eyes, "You must withdraw from the square."

Unarmed soldiers attempt to advance past demonstrators.

Jacques Langevin (Sygma)

Someone said, "If we leave, who will protect the students?"

Then I went to the west side of the monument and informed the students that the soldiers were not merely using clubs as they had imagined. "I saw with my own eyes many people being killed by guns," I said. "It's not worth sacrificing your lives at the hands of this kind of government. You must leave the square immediately."

I met Chai Ling and other student leaders at the monument. I repeated to them what I had told the students below. "You must retreat," I implored. "If you don't, no one will forgive you." I had an impulse to grab the microphone, but I managed to suppress it.

Chai Ling looked at me. She began to weep. She took the microphone and declared, "Fellow students, this is a peaceful sit-in. Everyone please remain seated and do not resist the army."

Then a young man came up to me and said angrily, "We'll kill anyone who makes us withdraw." We almost fought.

At this point several people came to us claiming to be soldiers. They all looked very nervous. They also wanted the students to withdraw.

Up to now, the people in the square had only heard rumors of bloodshed, which they shrugged off as mere hearsay. Even after I described what I had seen in great detail, some still didn't believe me. I went to the south side of the monument to warn the students there. I said in desperation, "If I cannot convince you to leave, I beg you to remain still. Do not resist. If you remain still, you might have a chance."

—*Cai Chongguo, a doctoral candidate*

We kept trying to tell the soldiers that no one wanted to start a revolt, that we were demonstrating against official corruption. We told them that if the government would open a direct dialogue with the students and city residents, then everything could be resolved. We linked our arms together and walked toward the soldiers singing the "Internationale." We hoped that their conscience would be awakened and they would retreat, but we were too naive. They suddenly opened fire at us—unarmed civilians!—with machine guns. The whole front row fell. I was paralyzed with fear. Everybody ran toward the Beijing Hotel and I ran with them, but I tripped and fell. I was sure it was the end and that I was going to be crushed. But when the shooting stopped, I found myself still intact.

The only thing in our minds was to rescue the wounded. Several rescue vehicles had tried to enter the square, but they had all failed. Then one of the No. 38 buses, which we later called the "heroic bus," succeeded in getting some of the wounded out. It had already lost three drivers; as the fourth drove up to Xiehe Hospital with the wounded, he slumped over the steering wheel and died.

—*Cao Xinyuan*

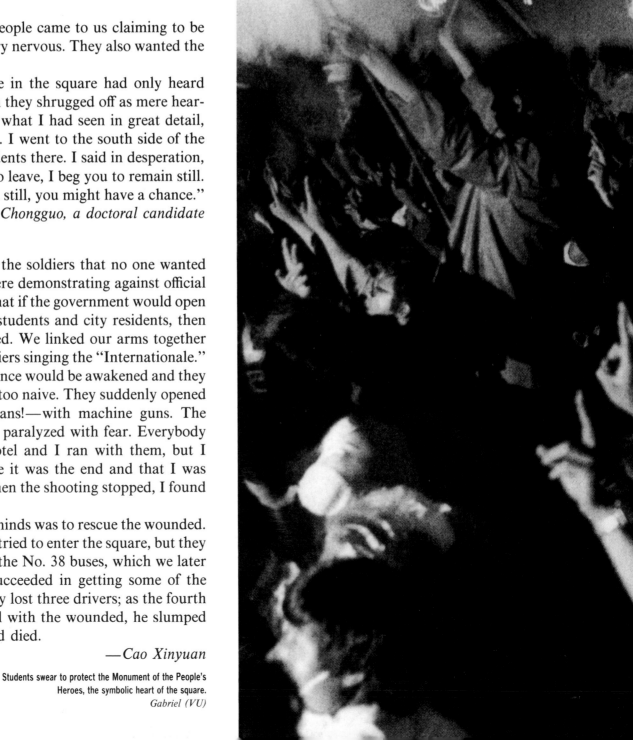

Students swear to protect the Monument of the People's Heroes, the symbolic heart of the square.
Gabriel (VU)

Mark Avery (AP)

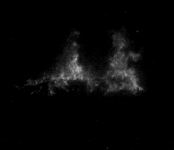

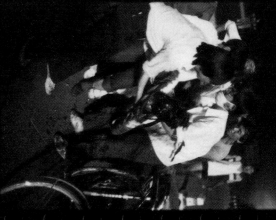

Gabriel

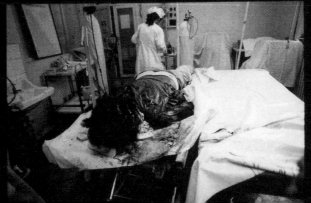

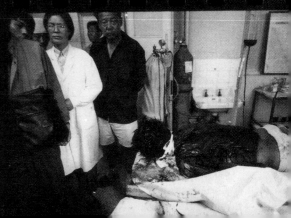

Jacques Langevin (Sygma)

"Four of my best friends died in my arms today," he said, "why don't you kill me, too?" He patted his chest. "Come on, open fire," he insisted.

By 1:00 A.M. the army had arrived at Xidan, spearheaded by armed police. They moved in a reversed-V formation, constantly throwing something at the crowds—it could have been tear gas. I was so shocked I didn't feel anything. People nervously moved aside to allow the army to pass. The troops advanced slowly as if fighting in the jungle. Many were shooting, sometimes into the air but more often at the crowds. When the armed police were about fifty-five yards away from the blockade, a courageous young man stood in the middle of the road holding high a red banner. As a bus behind him blazed violently, the man fell to the ground. The army was delayed by the fire but continued shooting at the crowds. I hid behind a bus ticket office. A young man next to me was gunned down. I couldn't see where he was shot, but he was covered with blood. Another young man asked if we should hide in nearby houses. We didn't move. He left alone, walking closely against a wall. At that moment a group of armed police rushed toward us with submachine guns and clubs. One of them tried to drive us away with a club, but he didn't hit us. About twenty of us ran to one of the houses for protection, leaving behind the poor man who had been shot.

The courtyard was full of people and the ground was sticky with blood. It was pitch dark. Inside the house we found that the man who had asked us to join him was lying in a pool of blood. I could feel that people were on the verge of going mad. Because of the tear gas, we couldn't keep our eyes open. Tears were streaming down our faces, and we cursed the soldiers. We made a stretcher from a board—which I tore off a telephone booth—and two iron bars and put the wounded man on it even though I thought he was already dead. We just needed to feel that there was something we could do. We ran with the stretcher, keeping close to the wall, toward a hospital near the Minzu Hotel.* The troops were lurid under the streetlights, their faces a terrifying red. They spotted us. Some of them fired at us, while others cheered.

Though army vehicles were still in sight, Beijing residents resurfaced by the thousands. Changan Avenue was packed with angry people. Everyone was weeping. They followed the troops and shouted "Bandits! Bandits!" The soldiers turned around and shot at them. As soon as the gunfire stopped, however, people removed the wounded and marched on.

Trails of bloodstains led me to two nearby hospitals. Through the window I saw the wounded on stretchers in the hallway and a doctor shaking his head from side to side.

—*Hou Tienming*

The Early Hours of June 4 as Recorded in the Notebook of Jan Wong, *Toronto Globe and Mail* Correspondent

01.00: Saw an armed personnel carrier go through the barricade at the Wangfujing/Changan intersection toward the square. It was stopped by the crowd just before Mao's portrait in the square.

01.15: People tried to roll buses out onto the street in front of the hotel.

01.18: The APC in the square is on fire.

01.20: Sound of gunfire coming from the area around Qianmen Gate.†

01.25: More gunfire from there.

02.15: Heavier gunfire.

02.16: Mass panic in the square (people flooding out). Ambulance stopped at Beijing Hotel to pick up man shot right outside the hotel.

02.20: Five ambulances pass the hotel on way to the square.

02.23: Five or six tanks came past the hotel from the east. Mass panic.

02.28: Five ambulances raced back to the square.

02.35: Intense gunfire from square. Mass panic again, crowds fleeing eastward. Two rows of troops march across Changan eastward from the square to seal it off, shooting as they go. Tens of thousands panic and run eastward.

02.39: Mass panic after more shooting.

02.40: Soldiers shoot some more. Crowd very dense so can't see bodies fall.

02.48: Man with red banner leads crowd back away from the square shouting "Retreat!"

02.50: Ambulance plows back into crowd, returning from the square.

From 02.35 to 02.48: Troops have cleared large portion of the square.

03.07: They start shooting at students who threw rocks at soldiers at the eastern end of the square.

03.12: Tremendous gunfire from the same spot. Vast crowd flees back to Beijing Hotel but is not allowed in through the barred gates.

At about 1:30 A.M. there was some fighting on the street southwest of the square. A large bus drove toward us from the southeast of Qianmen. The soldiers inside the bus hurled tear gas at the crowds of people assembled on the square. At first the people began to retreat, but they didn't go very far.

---

* The Minzu Hotel is west of the square, on Changan Avenue.

† Qianmen Gate is at the south end of Tiananmen Square.

Chinese Photographer Zong Hoi Yi
witnessed this extraordinary sequence. Angry
demonstrators isolate a PLA soldier . . .

MASSACRE
143

Beat him with stones, clubs, and sticks . . .

The bus stopped in the southwest corner of the square —the soldiers had run out of tear gas. Angry crowds rushed toward the vehicle showering it with bricks and stones. A mob shouting "One-two, one-two" tried to overturn the bus, but they couldn't quite push it over. They stopped, and some people got on the bus and began beating the soldiers with sticks. The news that other soldiers had already killed some people angered these Beijing citizens. A few college students and I shouted, "Don't beat them! Don't beat them!" But it was no use. We could see that the soldiers in the bus had no weapons. Many were beaten to death.

Someone dragged one soldier, who was still alive, out of the bus. People surrounded and attacked him. Four or five of us tried to use our bodies to protect this soldier. "Don't beat him! Don't beat him!" we yelled. "We don't want violence!"

A tall man looked at me indignantly and shouted, "They've killed our people!" Then someone jumped up and kicked the soldier. My glasses were suddenly knocked off; I couldn't see a thing. I could no longer help him. Miracu-

lously, after feeling around on the ground for a while, I found my glasses, intact.

The sound of gunfire came nonstop from the direction of Zhushikou.* Tracer bullets flashed one after another. I was in the pine tree grove to the west of Mao's mausoleum when I saw a Western reporter. "Some people have been beaten to death," I said. He held out three fingers and said in Chinese, "I saw three people killed at Zhushikou; their stomachs had been cut open."

From the south side of Qianmen and then through the southwestern intersection of the square came a contingent of air force troops. Their expressions were fierce and they looked ready to kill. They shouted a slogan from Chairman Mao: "We will not attack unless attacked; if attacked, we will certainly counterattack!"

Holding their semiautomatic weapons, which had been fitted with bayonets, the soldiers moved quickly toward the Great Hall of the People. When some people tried to block

---

* Zhushikou is located south of Tiananmen.

Students come to his aid . . .

them, the troops immediately fired warning shots above their heads. The people scattered, and the soldiers disappeared at the south entrance of the Great Hall.

On the west side of Qianmen, more than 1,000 airmen sat on the grass. They had received their marching orders, but because they hadn't fired on the people, the civilians and students in the area tried to persuade them not to use force. Some of the soldiers repeatedly opened the cartridges of their guns to show the crowd that they weren't loaded. But I saw others carrying heavy metal cases and flat green wooden boxes that obviously contained bullets.

The troops started to move toward the Great Hall of the People. Thousands of civilians and students now surrounded them, urging them not to shoot. Some women were crying desperately and pulling at the soldiers' hands, pleading with them to have mercy on the students. One student, his voice hoarse, accused the soldiers at Muxudi of slaughtering the students. Men and women, old and young—everyone—had tears in their eyes.

Some of the soldiers were clearly moved by the people's

pleas. One soldier tried to be reassuring: "Please don't worry; we'll never open fire on the people!"

The loudspeaker at the east entrance to the Great Hall of the People repeatedly broadcast the announcement that a counterrevolutionary rebellion was occurring in the capital. In the square, the atmosphere was haunting, and the smell of gunpowder filled the air.

—*Lao Gui*

At 2:00 A.M., June 4, I went to Nanchizi* to see what was going on. The students had no idea what was about to happen, but they were writing their wills on the steps of the monument. A graduate student from Qinghua University and another from a university in Xian tagged along with me.

Tanks had approached along Changan Avenue. The student guards prevented anyone from passing beyond the "Statue of Democracy," where soldiers stood facing the square, ready to charge. Machine guns were stationed on the

_____
* Nanchizi is a street to the east of Tiananmen.

Protect him from demonstrators . . .

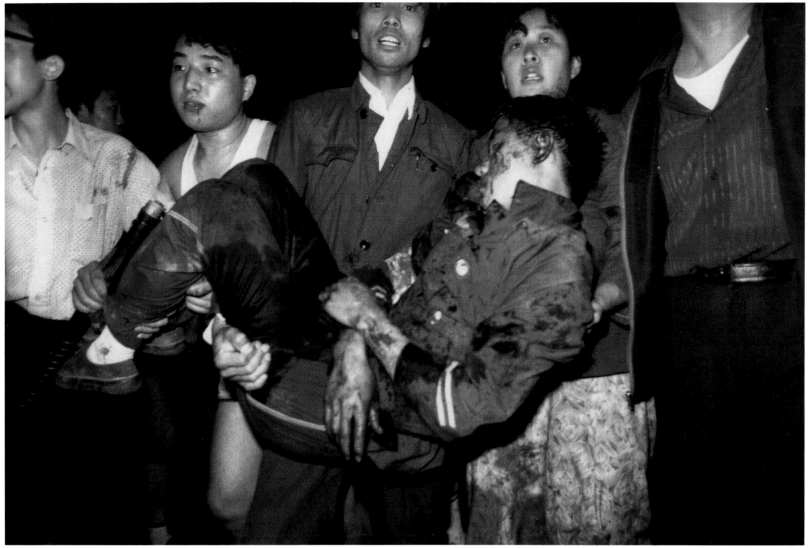
And carry him to safety.

roof of the Museum of Chinese History.* We could not go to Nanchizi via Changan Avenue, so we headed south.

Near Qianmen, we met a girl whose body was covered with blood. I asked if she was wounded but she said no. An old watermelon peddler had been bayoneted to death by a soldier; she had blood on her because she had tried to save the old man. She told us not to go in that direction because it was dangerous.

We got to Nanchizi using a detour. Army trucks were on the road and there was sporadic shooting. If someone in the crowd shouted "Fascists," the soldiers shot him.

People hid themselves in alleys and underground passes when the troops opened fire, but they ran out again when the soldiers stopped shooting. Some threw rocks or shouted slogans. Then the troops fired again, and three or four people fell. And the crowd dispersed again.

There was a girl twenty-three or twenty-four years old wearing a light pink dress. Her younger brother had been shot. Crying, she charged toward the soldiers with a cigarette. As I watched the girl run forward, I suddenly felt something like hot water splashing my face. I touched it; I

felt brains and blood. I looked around and found the two students who had come with me lying on the ground. They had been shot in the head; their faces were bloody. The one from Xian was alive. Although the student from Qinghua was not moving, one of his eyes was still open. It was full of horror.

When we were biking to Nanchizi, he had said to me, "If you look, Professor Yu, you'll see that the sky of Beijing is always slightly red." I thought he was still staring at the sky as he died.

—*Yu Shuo, professor of philosophy at People's University*

Whatever trust I had in the government went up in smoke with the gunfire. The People's Army was shooting at the people.

I hid off to the side and began to count the dead and wounded. From 2:10 to 3:05 A.M., I saw twenty-nine people carried away. The most terrible incident involved a girl and her brother. Soldiers had shot the brother from behind and were taking him away. His sister went absolutely mad when she saw this. She asked for a cigarette, lit it, and started to run toward the army trucks. People stopped her and tried to

---

* The Museum of Chinese History is next to Tiananmen Square on its eastern side.

tell her that the soldiers were not human anymore. She was quiet for a moment and puffed on her cigarette. Suddenly, she took off like a flash and ran toward the troops.

"It's a girl!" I shouted, hoping that the soldiers would not shoot at a woman. After all, she held only a cigarette, not a bomb. But they fired at her at point-blank range, leaving her soaked in her own blood. After a few seconds, we all broke down crying. Some people crawled into the line of fire and dragged the girl back, her body leaving a trail of blood. She was tall and dressed in a pink skirt, about twenty years old. She was finished, just like that.

A makeshift ambulance tried to enter the square to take the wounded away, but it was stopped by several rounds of gunshots that completely destroyed its windshield. A real ambulance was also stopped. With my own eyes I saw many people lying in their blood in the street. They should have been taken to hospitals immediately, but we weren't allowed into the square. I thought that, no matter what, we had to get those people out. But those who tried were pulled back by their friends. Off and on, the soldiers continued to shoot at the wounded.

—A Capital Steel Mill worker

I saw a bus with a Red Cross flag on it heading for the monument. Through the windows I could see the silhouettes of the medical assistants. People started to applaud when they saw that this makeshift ambulance was making headway without being fired at, but when it reached the middle of the square, it was suddenly sprayed with gunfire. I could see the bullets sparking as they hit the pavement. Everyone inside ducked. The bus stopped and stood for a long time in the middle of the vast expanse of the square like a ghost vehicle. After a time, it turned around again and left the square.

—Cha J., lecturer at People's University

At 2:05 A.M., I watched troops rush out from Tiananmen Gate in a barrage of gunfire. I saw several dozen people killed in front of me. My friend Chen Jing shouted, "Don't run! We have to retrieve the bodies." A little while later the troops massed in front of the Public Security Ministry while we all lined up in front of the Beijing Hotel, which was diagonally across Changan Avenue. Dead bodies were strewn in between. Civilians inched forward to haul away the bodies, but each time they did so, the soldiers fired on them. This happened time and again. Each time, more people fell.

People had stockpiled Molotov cocktails at every major intersection, and all traffic was completely blocked. When news came that night that the 38th Army would fight the 27th Army, every one of us prepared to help the 38th. But on the night of June 3, when the fighting around Xidan intensified, I and other members of the workers' federation

Another injured soldier
is protected by students.
Peter Charlesworth (JB Pictures)

02:35: Intense gunfire from square. Mass panic . . . crowds fleeing eastward. Troops march across Changan eastward, shooting as they go. . .

went to the student headquarters to ask for their weapons, which they refused to give us. If we had had weapons in Beijing, 30,000 or even 50,000 troops wouldn't have been a big deal to the people of Beijing.*

—*Tao Ye, member of the Workers' Union Federation*

Walking toward the northwest corner of the square, I saw with horror that the Workers' Autonomous Federation tent was up in flames. I ran toward it, thinking that I had to see whether any of the people I knew from the federation were lying there dead or wounded. There was nobody at all, and I soon saw why: about twenty-five yards away stood approximately 300 soldiers. All facing toward the tent. I

circled around to approach the tent from the back; the rising flames shed a bright light all around. As I climbed the parapet around the steps leading down to the pedestrian underpass, I saw the single figure of a young man wandering around inside the burning tent, looking somewhat lost, trying to gather up piles of documents that were lying on the ground. I climbed along the parapet toward him and told him to give me the documents, together with a student banner. "On behalf of 1.1 billion Chinese people," he said to me, "I thank you sincerely." It sounds almost corny, but with 300 soldiers staring straight at us, and flames rising up all around, it had more than a touch of poignancy about it. He asked me to take the stuff over to the Students' Union headquarters on the monument, which I did right away. I don't know what happened to the young man, I just left him standing there in the burning tent.

From the monument, I went back to the Statue of Democracy. At around 2:00 A.M., I suddenly noticed the first

* The 27th Army, from Inner Mongolia, was one of the units involved in the occupation of Beijing. Many believe they are responsible for the violence and brutality that occurred on June 3–4. In contrast, the 38th Army, which was permanently based in Beijing, was reported to have disagreed with orders to enforce martial law. In the days immediately after the massacre, it was rumored that these two armies would fight each other.

A traffic barrier is converted into an antitank device.

Koichi Imaeda (Magnum)

We were told that he was a hero. After being shot, he . . . threw himself in front of a flaming gunbarrel, to prevent other people from being shot.

column of troop trucks begin to enter the square, along the wall of the Forbidden City. They were moving very slowly and hesitantly. Groups of infantry escorted them in, at first only a thin line, but quickly increasing to a thick column, all of them wearing helmets and carrying assault rifles. Slowly, the realization was filtering through to me that all of this was for real—it wasn't a movie set.

Around 2:20 A.M., I headed back to the Workers' Federation tent; it was now just a smoldering ruin. Directly to the west, a line of troops had formed, extending back toward the Great Hall of the People. A small crowd of citizens and students had gone up to the soldiers, and some were even talking to them. But when I approached the line, the soldiers glared ferociously, leveled their guns, and waved at me to leave immediately. Before I did so, I took a good look at their faces. I was astonished at how young they looked—they seemed to be no more than sixteen years old, and some even looked as if they might be as young as fourteen. They were

extremely hard and vicious-looking. But they also seemed, I thought, to be quite frightened: their faces were flushed and reddened, and they were sweating profusely and breathing fast and heavily. Their steel helmets and uniforms looked way too big for them, but they held their rifles with a steady grip. The monument, several hundred yards distant, loomed sepulchrally through the eerie white light. Silence continued to reign on all sides, broken only by the occasional sound of gunfire from beyond the square and by the surreal echoing of the official broadcasts telling everyone over and over again to leave immediately, that the martial law troops were empowered to use any means necessary to clear the square. At that moment I thought that I was probably the only foreigner left in the square, and I was swamped by an aching sense of loneliness. There was also fear—but somehow surprisingly little. Basically, I knew I had to decide now, whether to stay or to leave—if, indeed, that was still possible. I decided I would stay. It was a straightforward decision

Armored personnel carriers (APC) encounter fierce civilian resistance.   *Jeff Widener (AP)*

Rei Ohara (Photo Shuttle: Japan)

Gabriel

Our sentiments swayed with those of the masses in the square. About 3:00 A.M. . . . fear reached its peak. No one could face the situation calmly anymore.

in the end: if all the journalists had already left (as I thought at that time), then someone, a foreigner, would have to remain to witness the impending events, to see how they "did" it.

—*Robin Munro*

I looked at my watch: it was 3:00 A.M. and the wounded were still coming in. There were college students, teachers, local residents, children, and elderly people.

Two students were brought in. Their friends had torn off their shirts and pants to tie up their bleeding thighs. Then there were five students from Beijing and Nanjing universities who were stuck together with their own blood when we pulled them out of the ambulance. Three of them were already dead, but we managed to save the other two. In tears, the nurses sent the bodies to the morgue. The emergency room was a mess; the floor was stained with blood, everyone was cursing and sobbing—we were all going insane.

People carried in a broad-shouldered worker who was about thirty years old. He had five wounds in his chest, his ribs were broken, and his thorax was gushing blood. An eyewitness told us that he was a hero. After being shot once,

instead of falling, he rushed forward and threw himself in front of a flaming gunbarrel to prevent other people from being shot. Finally, a soldier bayoneted him in the chest. Astonishingly, he was still conscious when he was brought in. He said he had a handicapped wife and a two-year-old child, and he pleaded with us to save him. We stitched him up and closed his thorax, but at 4:45 A.M. his pulse stopped.

At dawn, a seventy-four-year-old man was carried in. He had been shot in the head and was on the verge of death. His five-year-old grandson was by his side and kept pulling the old man's hand, crying, "Granddaddy, what's wrong with you?"

—*A Beijing doctor*

About 3:00 A.M., fear reached its peak. No one could face the situation calmly anymore. Our sentiments swayed back and forth with those of the masses in the square.

Gao Xin and Zhou Duo finally decided that the students and workers ought to be led out of the square. They came to seek the views of Liu Xiaobo and myself. Xiaobo was the only one who insisted on defending the square to the death. But, in the end, he gave in.

A bus is used to disrupt troop movement.

Peter Charlesworth (JB Pictures)

An APC tries to advance through a thick crowd.

Peter Charlesworth (JB Pictures)

We were still debating the issue when we heard Chai Ling's voice over the loudspeakers advising people that the final moment had come. She was saying that those who wished to could leave the square.

We sensed danger. If a lot of people decided to leave at once, the chaos might prompt the soldiers to act, to slaughter those who refused to leave. So we decided to try to persuade everyone to go.

We could already hear the sound of gunfire from the western side of the square coming nearer. Tear-gas shells were falling about fifty-five yards from us. There were still about 20,000 people gathered around the monument. We felt that their safety could only be assured if they moved off in a group. The question was how to persuade them to listen to us, especially those who had written their wills.

The student leaders raised two points: our duty to the citizens and students who had already given their lives, and how to deal with the retaliation that would inevitably follow after we abandoned the square.

There was still one broadcasting post functioning at that time. Li Lu or Feng Congde—I'm not sure which—led us to the microphone and introduced us to the crowd. We appealed to them to lay down anything that might be regarded as a weapon. There was one machine gun, two semiautomatic rifles, a pistol, and a box of Molotov cocktails.

A group of workers was manning a machine gun at the top of a flight of steps. The workers tensed when they saw us approach. I embraced a young man, perhaps in his early twenties, and told him I was Hou Dejian. "Brother Hou!" He called out, then he cried. He said that many of his companions had already been killed in an effort to stop the military trucks and to protect the students. He himself was also wounded. I cried, too, embracing him tightly. It was the first time in many years that I had cried.

We told the workers that if the PLA discovered the machine gun we would all die without being given the chance to explain ourselves. They agreed to remove the machine gun and then led us to another tent, where they produced a rifle that had no ammunition.

Liu Xiaobo took the weapons to a group of reporters and destroyed them while the reporters took photographs. Other students started throwing down their weapons, too.

Two doctors from the Red Cross suggested that we approach the troops in an ambulance and negotiate with them in the hope that they would promise to let us withdraw from the square. Zhou Duo and I decided to go while Xiaobo and Gao Xin stayed to collect the weapons and reassure the students.

When we reached the corner of the square we saw a mass of troops. We got out of the ambulance and ran toward them. As we approached, we heard the clicking of rifles and

Jacques Langevin (Sygma)

A bulldozer disappears under a tank's treads.

Jacques Langevin (Sygma)

the troops shouted to us to stop.

Their political commissar, Colonel Ji Xinguo, listened to our request and then asked us to put an end to our hunger strike. We replied that we had already done so. Then, in a very gentle manner, the officer said he had to consult headquarters. Within five minutes of his leaving us, the lights in the square went out. We were very frightened. The soldiers were impatient. Some clicked their guns, some shouted, others stamped on the broken bottles that littered the area. The four of us stood there, not daring to move. The doctors called on the troops to hurry.

Finally Colonel Ji reappeared and told us that headquarters had agreed to our request, and that the safest route for withdrawal was the southeast.

We raced back to the monument. I said I knew that those still in the square were not afraid to give their lives. But if we were to die there, we would have committed an unpardonable sin against the country. The struggle for democracy would not be won quickly. The movement had already enjoyed great success. We were already victorious.

The sound of gunfire got louder as I spoke. Students were cursing me. I couldn't hear them clearly, but I guessed they were accusing me of giving in.

I shouted back, "Blame me, curse the four of us, but leave the square safely."

The sentiment in the square began to change, but the sound of gunfire was getting nearer. I saw soldiers closing in from the south, in trucks and on foot. I was concerned that this would shake the students' belief in the commissar's promise. I asked Zhou Duo and the two doctors to ask the army for more time.

Then the troops stationed on the northern side began to move. We found Colonel Ji in the middle of the square. He was deadly serious. He said he had heard our speech but that the troops had to carry out their orders to clear the square.

He said that if we could not persuade the students to get out, we four had better go first. We vowed that we would be the last ones to leave the square. If we were afraid of death, we would have left long ago, we declared.

A soldier standing nearby went red in the face from shouting and pointed his gun at us. We realized there was nothing more to be said.

"Run to the southeast!" we called as we raced back to the monument. A dozen soldiers had already reached the top

We could hear gunfire coming nearer. Tear-gas shells were falling about fifty-five yards from us. 20,000 people were still gathered around the monument . . .

and shot out the loudspeakers. By now there was gunfire everywhere.

The crowd around the monument quickly dispersed. I signaled to a group of soldiers to point their guns toward the sky, and some of them did. They shouted my name and asked me to leave quickly.

I stood on the first flight of steps and watched the students lining up, banners held high, and moving slowly toward the southeast. I heard them calling to me, "Come with us."

I waved to them, and then with two sentries and Zhou Duo headed toward the northeast part of the square. People were still sitting on the ground there. Zhou Duo and I pulled them up whenever we could. "Blame me, curse me if you like, but move!" we said. Some extended their hands without saying a word. Others stood up and explained, "Teacher Hou, we don't blame you."

"Thank you," I cried aloud as I pulled at them.

Before the last group of students arose, troops pressed us from the west in a human wall. They moved in quickly and squeezed us like water in the neck of a bottle, barely able

to move. I could hardly breathe.

All around me plainclothes antiriot police were waving thick wooden sticks and beating people on their heads and bodies.

Students were bleeding. The crowd stumbled over iron railings that had been scattered on the ground. A whole row of people fell. Those behind fell over them, and the next wave over them.

—*Hou Dejian, a Taiwanese singer who defected to the mainland in 1983*

From a live tape recording made by a German journalist of the last hours before the shooting at the monument

[Sound of tanks rumbling in the background]
Male voice: Don't be a sucker.
[Noise of the crowd swells]
Government broadcast: The Beijing municipal government and martial law headquarters urgently announce that

Changan Avenue in the early morning hours of June 4.   *Jacques Langevin (Sygma)*

counterrevolutionary rebellion is now taking place. Ruffians are violently attacking PLA soldiers, confiscating arms and ammunition, burning army vehicles, setting up roadblocks, and kidnapping soldiers. They aim to overthrow the People's Republic of China—to overthrow the Socialist system. PLA soldiers have shown a great deal of restraint in the past several days. Now we must crack down on this counterrevolutionary turmoil. All Beijing citizens should observe martial law and cooperate with the PLA to protect our laws and our great Socialist motherland. All citizens and students now in the square should leave immediately and let the troops carry out their tasks. We cannot guarantee the safety of those who disregard our advice. They will be completely responsible for anything that happens to themselves. . . . The Beijing municipal government and martial law headquarters urgently announce . . .

[Sound of breaking bottles and whistling]

Male voice: He was hit by a bullet!

Second male voice: A bullet? A *real* bullet?

First male voice: Yes, a real bullet!

Second male voice: A real bullet? Where?

Female voice: Is it real?

Second male voice: Yes! The signs are full of bullet holes.

First male voice: Let's get out of here.

Student broadcast: Fellow students. We bear a historic responsibility. We must decide for ourselves whether to defend the monument. We should stop those who are trying to resist the army. Stop anyone trying to fight back.

All students guarding the square, please return to the monument. We must protect the monument. Protect our banners of democracy.

[The sound of a siren from an approaching ambulance]

Voices: Get out of the way! Get out of the way!

Student broadcast: Liu Xiaobo, Zhou Duo, and Gao Xin urgently call upon the army to stop using their machine guns and bayonets to slaughter unarmed civilians. Our principles are nonviolent. Our hunger strike was a peaceful and lawful means to express our discontent. We protest the imposition of martial law. But, now, too much blood has been shed. This cannot continue. We implore you to send representatives to the monument to negotiate with us, immediately. We will take responsibility for persuading the students to leave the square. . . .

Voices singing: The Internationale must be realized. We have never had a savior or a saintly king. We must depend on ourselves to create a humane society.

Hou Dejian: Students, citizens, **[applause]** we have already shed a lot of blood.

Male voice: Please be quiet!

June 4, dawn. Changan Avenue.
Jacques Langevin (Sygma)

We all broke down crying. . . . She was tall and dressed in a pink skirt, about twenty years old. She was finished, just like that.

Hou: We cannot remain here anymore. Students and citizens, I dare to say that our movement has succeeded, **[cheers and applause]** but we have not won today. Students, all the people here now are outstanding citizens of China. **[applause]** None of us fears death, but our deaths should serve some purpose. Speaking on behalf of four of us who are hunger-strikers, we didn't consult with you students for your permission to take a certain action. A moment ago we went to the north side of the square to talk to the soldiers. We found their commander. We were hoping that no more blood had to be shed. We spoke with the political commissar of troop 51048, Colonel Ji Xinguo, and he reported to the command post of the martial law forces. We all agreed that all citizens of the People's Republic of China should leave the square in safety.

Male voice: No! No!

Zhou Duo: Students! If we can save even one more drop of blood now, there will be that much more hope for the future of our march toward democracy.

[Sound of tanks passing]

Male voice: Please be quiet!

Zhou: We have agreed to lead the students away from the square as quickly as possible. The soldiers told us that they have orders from their commanders to clear the square before dawn. That means they are going to use any means necessary.

Students, we cannot use fists against soldiers armed with rifles and bayonets. There are no more conditions for further negotiations. We must now try our best to save ourselves. They have agreed to leave a path at the southern corner of the square for us to withdraw. We hope we can withdraw in an orderly, safe manner, at once.

Liu Xiaobo: If we want to achieve democracy, we must start now, with ourselves. The minority should listen to the majority. That is a basic principle of democracy.

Hou Dejian: Friends, no matter what you think about what I have done, I hope we can leave safely and peacefully. I personally shall remain in the most

A demonstrator is beaten. Taken by a Chinese photographer, this image was smuggled out of China by American photojournalists.

Anonymous (Black Star)

The soldiers told us that they have orders . . . to clear the square before dawn. . . . We cannot use fists against soldiers armed with rifles and bayonets.

dangerous place of all until the last of you have left.

[Applause]

Liu Xiaobo: What Hou just said represents the wishes of all four of us. We will stay until the last one of you leaves.

First male voice: What's wrong with these guys?

Second male voice: You Fascist running dogs!

Male voice (over loudspeaker): They've stabbed the people in the back. If we stay, we'll die needlessly. Some students want to stay because they have delusions about the government not using force on them. But it's absurd to risk our lives. We should preserve our forces. Now, I beg you to withdraw from the square immediately.

Liu Xiaobo (over loudspeaker): Let's hold each other's hands. Let's be quiet and think about the situation carefully, and about what we should do next. The decision on whether to leave or not depends on everyone here.

Male voice: If we must die, let's die together!

Liu: Students! Students! Throughout the movement, the citizens of Beijing and the workers gave us great support. We cannot win the movement without their support. Now I'm sure the students in the square can leave together safely, but I cannot guarantee the citizens' safety. At this important moment, I appeal to all the students to try your best to protect the citizens and leave the square from the south corner in an orderly manner.

Male voice: Hurry, let's go!

Another male voice: Sit down!

Third male voice: Point your guns at us! Go ahead!

[The "Internationale" is sung]

Chanting crowd: The People's army does not fight the people! The People's army does not fight the people!

Male voice: If I had a gun, I would not be afraid to use it.

Student broadcast: Soldiers and officers, you are the sons of the people! Don't point your guns at the people!

Crowd: Don't point your guns at the people!

Male voice: What are they doing?

[Gunfire]

One of the official photographs of the Tiananmen incident distributed by Xinhua, China's preeminent press agency.

Li Jin (Xinhua)

Male voice: They're shooting at the loudspeakers!
Another male voice: Those are real bullets!
Third male voice: Don't shoot at the monument!
Crowd: Don't shoot at the monument!
Female voice: Don't shoot at the monument! . . .
Male voice: Protect yourselves—they're going to fire tear gas!
[Sound of tanks and gunfire]
Male voice: Drag her! Pull her into line!
Another male voice: They're going to hit us. Stop it! Stop!
Male voice: I told them to leave their tents. They wouldn't follow my advice.
[The "Internationale"; machine-gun fire; screaming]
Male voice: Let's hold each other tightly.
[The "Internationale"]
Female voice: Don't panic!
Another male voice: Don't push! Don't push!
Male voice: Don't hit people. Don't hit people!
[Cursing; a babble of different dialects]
Male voice: Don't panic!
Another voice: My glasses!
Male voice: Let's go! Let's go!
Male voice: Stop pushing, stop pushing . . . I'm falling!

At 3:00 A.M., I met up with an American journalist named Richard Nations. At 4:00 A.M., all the lights went out; we ran back from the north side of the square to the side with the monument.

Through the dim gloom, I suddenly noticed the figure of a young man standing about two yards away from me. There was something vaguely disturbing about him, so I looked more carefully. He was standing completely still, legs spread slightly apart; one arm was stretched out, holding some kind of object. His eyes looked somehow crazy. I looked down and saw that he was carrying a Molotov cocktail, gripping it tightly by the neck of the bottle. I went over to him and said, "No, the students don't want you to do anything like that." He just stared back at me, not saying anything. After the lights had gone out in the square, the students' loudspeakers on the monument began to crackle, and a voice announced slowly, almost as if announcing a railway schedule: "We will now play the 'Internationale.' We will now play the 'Internationale.'" The crackling sound suddenly increased, filling the silence all around, as the record was put on. The music began at full volume. As the lyrics soared out from the monument through the darkness ("The final battle is upon us, unite until the morrow, the Internationale will surely be achieved"), and with the students still all sitting there, completely motionless and utterly resolute, I found myself thinking: what are all those thousands of soldiers feeling right now, sitting there in the dark, their eyes focused on this incredible scene? The record ended. It was played again immediately, and then again a

Bicycle carts, normally used to make deliveries,
are commandeered to aid the wounded.
Jacques Langevin (Sygma)

The last body was a young man on top of a flattened bicycle. He had been trying to climb over the bicycles to get away from the tank. His head was crushed . . .

couple of times more. As it played, I was riveted by the sight of several young couples, well dressed, as they would be for a Sunday afternoon excursion somewhere, walking calmly, hand-in-hand, straight toward the monument. I had the overwhelming certainty that all these young people were determined to make history, that they would not flinch from the final moments of fear. With equal certainty, I knew that the attack would begin at any moment. They were going to do it, now. Then a grand array of lights suddenly came on all across the front of the Great Hall of the People. They looked like some kind of fairy lights on a Christmas tree—a brilliant but soft, luminous glow spreading all around the west side of the square. It was somewhere just after 4:30. There were by now very few citizens standing in the open in the square—only the 3,000 or so students, huddled all over the monument. And beyond it the great, wide spaces of the square itself, studded with the forlorn shapes of the abandoned tents and the miscellaneous debris of the encamp-

ment. Suddenly the loudspeakers on the monument crackled back into life. An unidentified student leader insisted that the students should on no account abandon the square: "We will now pay the highest price possible, for the sake of democracy in China." A leader of the Workers' Autonomous Federation then declared, "We must all leave here immediately, for a terrible bloodbath is about to take place. We must not let ourselves be slaughtered here senselessly." But everyone just continued sitting there as before; there was no sound at all. Hou Dejian then delivered a similar speech. He said, "We have already won a great victory. But now we have to go."

Richard and I decided to make a last trip up onto the monument, to pay our last respects. There was no hysteria among the students. My gut feeling was, rather, that everyone present knew perfectly well why he or she was there. There was no need for any further comment; all that was left now was to wait.

As we left the monument, hurrying to get clear of the

On the campus of a Beijing university.

Wu Yue (VU)

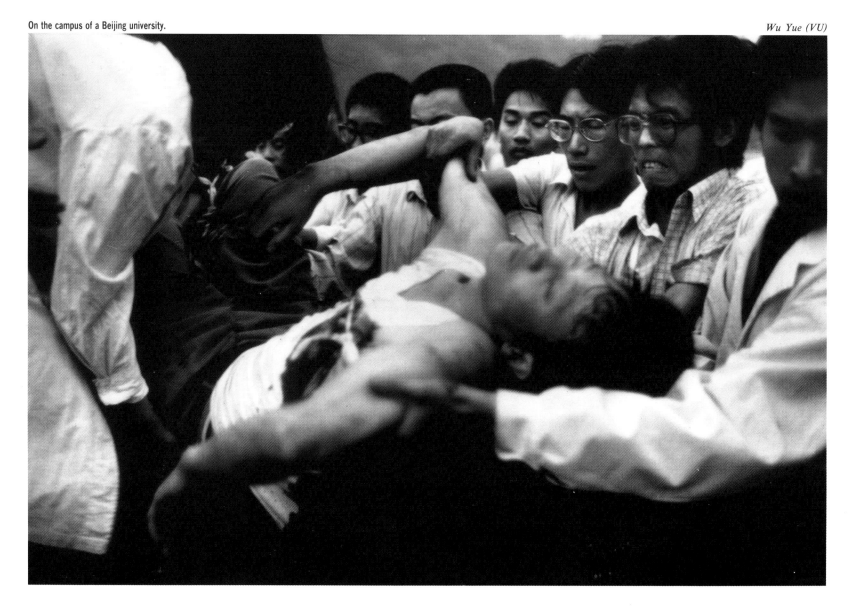

He said he had a handicapped wife and a two-year-old child, and he pleaded with us to save him. We . . . closed his thorax, but at 4:45 A.M. his pulse stopped.

direct line of fire, I felt hundreds of eyes boring into my back. Not a single person got up to leave. We took a position about twenty-five yards to the southeast of the monument. A distant, rumbling growl sounded from somewhere up in the northern sector of the square: the tanks had started up their engines. Minutes passed. Then someone—I don't know who—took the microphone and proposed a vote. It was a stroke of genius, and it undoubtedly saved the lives of hundreds if not thousands of innocent and defenseless people. Some moments later a mild and halfhearted shout went up around the square—by no means a majority of those present. That's all I heard: just the one shout. Then a voice came up over the loudspeaker saying that the democratic decision had been in favor of leaving. Slowly, people began to stand up and to make their way down the steps and off the monument. They had tears rolling down their cheeks, men and women alike. All looked shaken, and many were trembling badly or walking unsteadily; but all looked proud and un-

beaten. One small, dumpy, middle-aged woman, dressed in a white medical tunic and with her face mask still dangling around her neck, caught my attention in particular: she was weeping uncontrollably and being helped along by some students. I went up to her and took her by the hand, saying, "There's no shame in this, none at all, it's a great victory." Through her sobs she said, with deepest feeling, "No, there's no shame. We've done all we possibly could. Yes, it is a victory!"

Glancing northward at around 5:00 A.M., I suddenly realized that the Goddess of Democracy statue was no longer there. Richard and I headed quickly toward the north end of the square to take a look, half-running through the abandoned student encampment. As we rounded one tent and entered a more open area, a stunning sight met our eyes: about twenty-five yards away, a long row of armored vehicles was moving very slowly down through the square toward the monument, a dense line of troops following just

A Beijing hospital. *Gabriel (VU)*

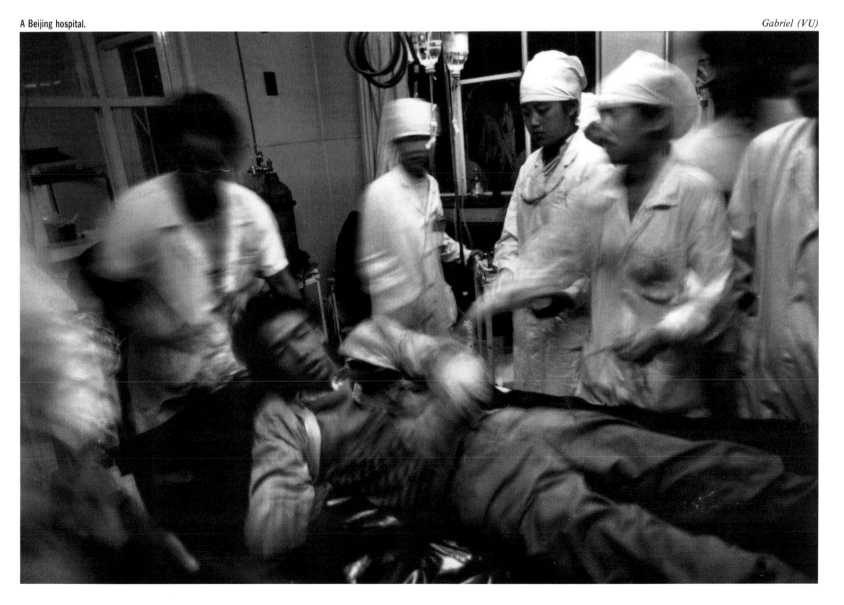

David Neil Berkwitz

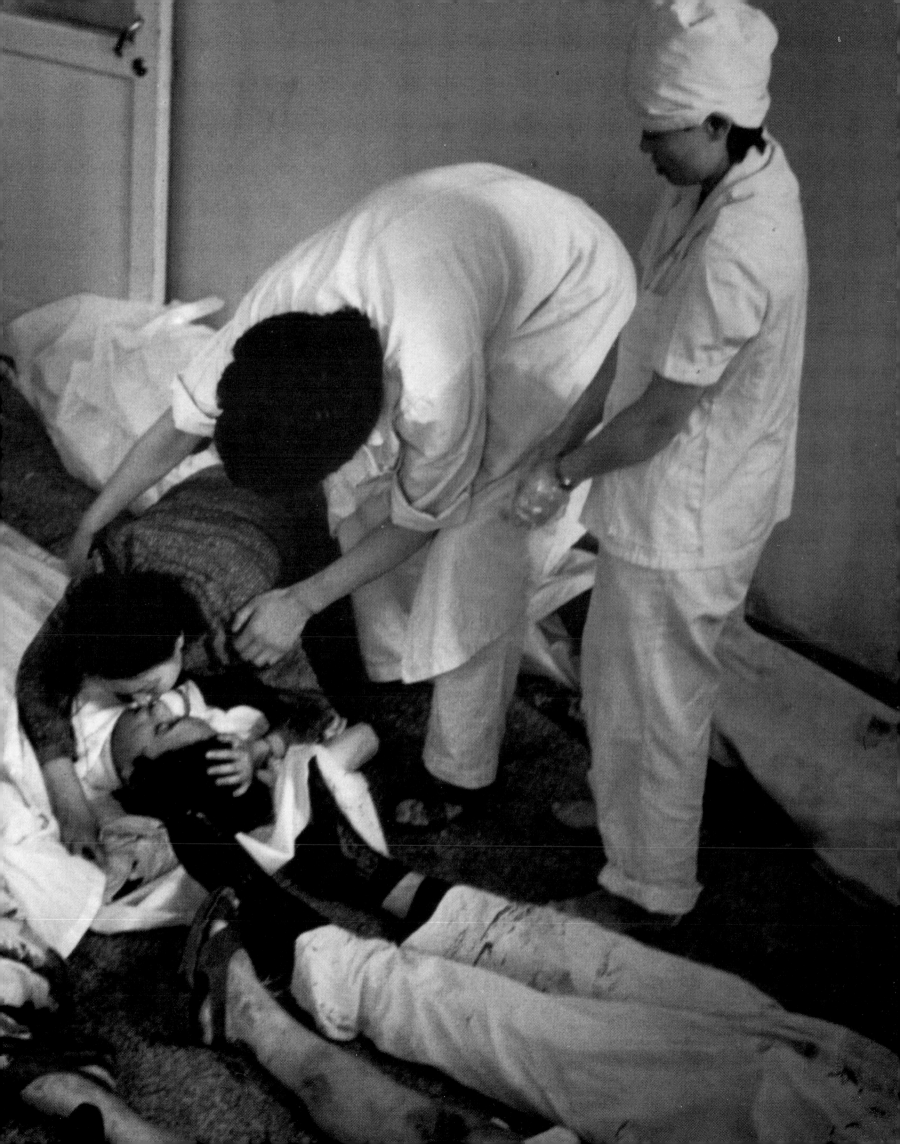

behind it. The tanks and APCs were simply crushing every-thing in their path—tents, railings, boxes of provisions, bi-cycles—all were knocked over and squashed flat in a slow-motion display of random military might. There were no soldiers to the front of the armored vehicles; they were all to the rear, and no one checked the tents. For all the tank drivers knew, the tents could have been full of ill or ex-hausted students. In actual fact, there were very few left inside, but it is likely that some were crushed to death.

We returned to the monument. The student evacuation was still under way, and the troops had already occupied the top level of the base. We remained in the square until 6:15 A.M., by which time the students and all but fifty or so of the citizens had left. One group of departing students had gone by with a platform-cart bearing a shiny blue printing ma-chine, the hand-cranked kind, lovingly wrapped in a box with newspaper all around it. Richard asked them, "Would you rather have a rifle or a printing press?"

"What good is the rifle?" they replied.

—*Robin Munro*

In fact, there was no conflict between the students and the troops. It was a peaceful retreat, and the students were calm. Some have said that when the students left the square they ran like crazy, and that some were even trampled to death. But this is only a rumor. Because many students were crowded together on the monument, it was a little chaotic for a moment, but then order was quickly restored.

The student guards were the last to leave. They fre-quently urged the students in front to walk faster and not to stop. Armed soldiers were walking about eighteen feet be-hind them, complaining constantly that the students were

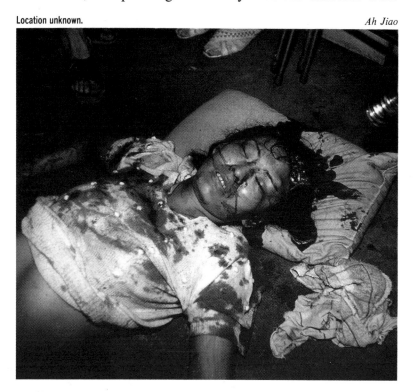

Location unknown.   *Ah Jiao*

The corner of a Beijing hospital.
Dario Mitidieri (Select)

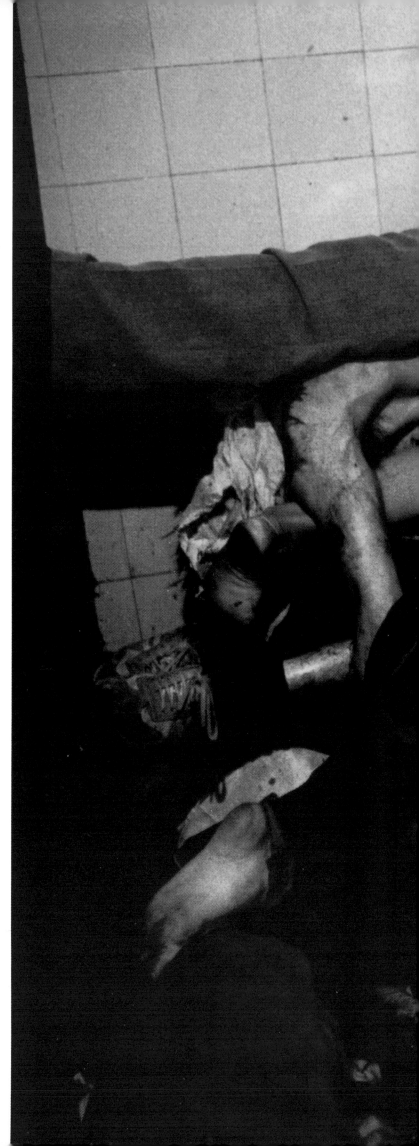

This was our first encounter with soldiers since leaving the square, so we couldn't contain our anger. We chanted "Beasts! Murderers!"

walking too slowly. They repeatedly fired warning shots at a forty-five-degree angle above the students' heads, forcing them to move faster. When the students reached the northeast side of Mao's mausoleum, a few APCs arrived from the north, charging toward the students at full speed, suddenly stopping just before they reached them, forcing the students to retreat quickly. I didn't see anyone get run over, luckily.

It was already light by the time the students passed the east side of Qianmen. I saw many air force troops sitting on the ground on the west side of Qianmen. Over and over, the students yelled at them "Deng Xiaoping is a butcher! Beast! Fascist!" At first the soldiers didn't react, but then they all stood up and got into marching formation. They moved quickly to the east and fired shots in the air. Students and civilians fled to the south, leaving the square.

—Lao Gui

I did not realize that I was the last one left at the monument. As I walked down the terrace, I saw a line of big characters on the relief: "June 4, 1989, the Chinese people shed blood and died for democracy." Beneath it read: "Written at 4 o'clock in the morning." As I turned around, I saw a soldier about to stab a bed with his bayonet. I saw two feet and remembered the story about an old man being bayoneted to death. I rushed forth and dragged the feet. A boy fell down from the bed. He was the last student to leave the square. The two of us walked down and met Liu Xiaobo at the second level of the monument. He suddenly asked a student about his bag.

The student replied, "Damn! I left it in the tent!" Liu's passport and all my manuscripts were in it. I said I would go back and get it. I walked back with my hands up. I thought they would not shoot me because the officer I talked to was sympathetic. A girl wanted to come along with me and she ran to catch up. The soldiers got very nervous and fired at the marble steps. The students who had withdrawn turned their heads back and looked at us. More than ten soldiers came over and fired a round of shots into the sky. I realized that it was impossible to go back and get the passport.

Liu would have been able to leave China had he had his passport. He would not have been arrested. He was very unfortunate.

It was five o'clock when I got to Mao Memorial Hall. Fifteen minutes had passed. When I looked at the square again, the tents were all flattened. Tanks and TV cameras were at work. It was such a contrast. I was so used to the red banners and tents, and suddenly they were all gone. As I thought of the students in the tents, I sat on the ground and

began to cry. . . . Zhang Gong, the spokesman for the martial law troops said that they had checked every tent. But how could they have checked more than 200 tents in just fifteen minutes?

—Yu Shuo

As we withdrew from the square, at about 5:00 A.M., we passed Qianmen. Local residents, young and old, male and female—some in their pajamas—lined the streets, applauding us tearfully. It was the first time in my life I had ever seen people applauding without cheering. It was a very strange and haunting scene. People standing in front shook the hands of every passing student. Very few words were exchanged; people communicated with their eyes. I noticed that some of the workers, who were unaccustomed to shaking hands, patted the students on their shoulders.

A middle-aged worker tightly embraced a student from Tianjin* and said, "You guys are great. We will never forget you."

The student cried and said, "This is my first trip to Beijing. I can't believe I ran into this!"

Some students held blood-soaked shirts over their heads to show the residents.

As we moved out of the residential area and headed toward Liubukou intersection, few civilians met us along the road. Someone advised, "You'd better run. And get rid of all those signs and banners. Who knows what has happened in your school district. There might be soldiers waiting for you with machine guns."

I was last in the line of Qinghua students. Behind us were students from the University of Law and Politics. When we arrived at Changan Avenue we saw about four rows of tanks stationed 300 feet east of the intersection. This was our first encounter with soldiers since leaving the square, so we couldn't contain our anger. We chanted "Beasts! Beasts! Murderers! Murderers!"

I saw the first row of tanks, four of them, begin its charge. The one on the north side of the street led the attack and they quickly picked up speed.

The students began to run in a panic—the ones in front of me ran north, while the ones behind me ran south. I ran north and quickly turned west but had trouble running because I was pushing my bike. The tanks kept gaining on us. I remembered someone screaming at me to hurry up. Another student helped me drag my bike onto the curb.

The tank missed me by a few yards. As it passed, the soldiers inside opened the hatch and tossed out four gas

---

* Tianjin is a city southeast of Beijing.

The early morning hours of June 4.
(Reuters-Bettmann Archive)

canisters. Unlike the gas canisters they had used the day before, which had made us cry, these containers spewed yellow fumes and choked us by irritating our lungs. Students retaliated by throwing rocks and bricks at the tanks. The tank advanced fifty-five yards, stopped, turned around, and headed for us again.

In the midst of this confusion I heard people screaming and saw them scattering madly in all directions. Those who ran past us yelled, "Someone has been crushed!" I quickly walked over to where the screams were first heard. The tank passed again.

Back up the street, about a dozen students had been trapped by burned buses and abandoned bicycles. They had been unable to escape the first charge of the tanks. The first body I saw was a girl dressed neatly in a white blouse and red skirt. She lay face down on the avenue. One of her legs was completely twisted around, the foot pointed up toward the sky.

Another, a male student, had his right arm completely severed from his shoulder, leaving a gaping black hole. The last body in the line of students was a young man on top of a flattened bicycle. He had been trying to climb over the bicycles to get away from the tank. His head was crushed: a pool of blood and brain lay on the pavement a few feet away.

Altogether, eleven students were crushed by this tank. Ten minutes later, an ambulance arrived and picked up three or four students who may still have been alive.

Most of the onlookers were young men from the neighborhood. A young couple who lived nearby came out of their house; the woman was screaming like a wounded animal. I have never heard a sound as painful as that. The man, in his thirties, was crying uncontrollably. The students, for the most part, had already fled. The citizens didn't dare curse the soldiers to their faces, cursing them instead as they stared at the dead bodies.

"Fuck you. Don't let me find any of you alone," warned one man.

"You haven't killed enough people? Machine guns weren't strong enough? Now you have to use tanks?"

I remained there for ten minutes, paralyzed from the shock of having witnessed this scene. I walked away without saying a word. Somehow I found myself at Xidan, but I could not remember having walked there. My only memory was of weaving around pools of blood here and there.

I met a couple in their thirties. "Have you just come from Tiananmen Square?" the woman asked me.

"Yes," I said.

"Turn your shirt inside out," she cautioned me.

My T-shirt had Qinghua University printed across the front. I did as she told me. At that moment, I desperately needed someone to show some understanding, and this woman's simple words and sympathetic eyes impressed me

The vehicles were apparently abandoned by PLA units and later burned by civilians.

so deeply that I almost cried. I'll never forget her.

—*Liu Tang*

From an article in the September 19, 1989, issue of *The People's Daily* **entitled "Martial Law Officers Ji Xinguo and Gu Benxi say, 'The Students Withdrew Peacefully, No Deaths Occurred.' "**

Colonels Ji Xinguo and Gu Benxi formally announced that during the whole process of clearing the square—except when soldiers shot at the loudspeakers on the monument, which were controlled by the Autonomous Student Union—no one fired at citizens and students. There were no deaths in the square.

Ji said that soldiers advanced with clubs in their hands,

Those butchers are not afraid of obvious exaggerations. Under the pretense of "verifying facts," they use one truth to cover up ten lies. They use the fact that no one was killed when they cleared the square to conceal the fact that before the square was cleared, people were injured and killed. They use the fact that there was no bloodbath in Tiananmen to conceal the bloodbaths at Muxudi, Nanchizi, and Liubukou. Why should we allow them to conceal the truth?

—*Lao Gui*

The toppling of the "Goddess of Democracy," was seen by millions of TV viewers around the world. Pushed by a tank, it fell forward and to the right, so that its hands and the torch struck the ground first, breaking off. It must have been quickly and easily reduced to rubble, mixing with all the other rubble in the square, to be cleared away by the army as part of its show of cleanliness and order. The statue, however, could not be so easily destroyed. It was intended from the beginning to be ephemeral, and yet to endure as an image of the desire of the great mass of Chinese people for the ideals it symbolized. I envision a day when a replica, as large as the original and more permanent, stands in Tiananmen Square, with the names of those who died there written in gold in its base. It may well stand there after Chairman Mao's mausoleum has, in its turn, been pulled down.

—*Cao Xinyuan*

David C. Turnley (Black Star)

keeping a distance from the withdrawing students. Before the troops got too close to them, the students began to retreat. As the troops advanced, the students' withdrawal sped up. Finally, a few students remained at the north side of the monument and troops had to force them out.

Gu said that before the armored personnel carriers came in, officers and soldiers checked every tent to see whether there was anyone inside. He checked the tents himself and saw a soldier take a crippled man out of the tent. A female student fainted because she was frightened. Soldiers took her out. When every tent had been checked and no one remained inside, APCs entered the square.

When troops came close to the monument, Gu and Ji said some students lost their senses, shouting counterrevolutionary slogans, cursing the troops, and throwing stones and soda bottles at the commanders and soldiers. If the troops hadn't exercised restraint in asking soldiers to carry out their orders, it would have been hard to avoid bloodshed and death.

AFTERMATH

I f the PLA had not entered the city, the students would have occupied the political heart of China —Tiananmen—and created endless incidents, spreading throughout the country.

One day, they built a so-called "Goddess of Liberty," the next day they got the intellectual circle to stage a so-called limited hunger strike. They collected a handful of hooligans to form a so-called volunteer army, death squads, and a group of "Flying Tigers."* The evidence indicated that only when the PLA smashed the counterrevolutionary rebellion in Beijing would the situation in China stabilize.
—*Yuan Mu, official spokesman of the State Council*

On the morning of June 4, I watched the students withdrawing from Tiananmen carrying the flags of Beijing University, Qinghua University, and other, out-of-town schools. There were two well-organized groups, with 400 or 500 members each. They shouted "Down with Li Peng!" and "Blood must be paid with blood!"

These were the survivors. Chai Ling and Feng Congde led them. They looked sad, but they maintained strict discipline, marching in ranks, hand in hand. Some were covered with grime.

Black banners hung from the front gate of Beijing University. One read: "The blood will enrich China's soil; the terrible scene we witnessed has never been seen before in human society." Emblazoned in bold red characters on post-

* The Flying Tigers were a group of citizens on motorcycles who traveled around the city alerting citizens to troop movements, etc., in the manner of Paul Revere.

Curious pedestrians
inspect an abandoned tank.
Zong Hoi Yi (VU)

ers hanging on the gate were the words: "We promise that we will repay this blood-debt."

Despite the government's efforts to black out news coverage, we listened to the BBC and VOA every day. The BBC rebroadcast this message from the China International Radio Station:

> This is Radio Beijing. Please remember June 3, 1989. The most tragic event has taken place in the Chinese capital. Thousands of people, most of them innocent civilians, were killed by armed soldiers who forced their way into the city. Among those killed were some of our colleagues from Radio Beijing. The soldiers used machine guns against local residents and students who tried to block their way. Even after the military convoys broke through their blockades, soldiers continued to spray bullets indiscriminately at crowds in the street. Eyewitnesses claim that some armored vehicles even ran down infantrymen who hesitated to fight the civilians. Radio Beijing's English Department mourns those who died in the tragic incident and appeals to its listeners to join our protest at this gross violation of human rights and at this most barbarous oppression of the people. Because of the abnormal situation here in Beijing, there is no other news we can bring you. We sincerely ask for your understanding and thank you for joining us at this most tragic moment.

Radio Beijing used English, so people were convinced that the news was true. During the following three days, the anchors of CCTV dressed all in black. In the midst of one broadcast, an anchorwoman broke into tears while she was talking about a flood in Guangdong that claimed seven lives. We all knew why she was really crying. After June 7, no announcers at all appeared on TV; the news was just printed across the screen.

—A Beijing teacher

At 9:00 A.M. on June 4, we returned to Beijing Normal University. Tens of thousands of people, young and old, were lined up along the streets, tearfully watching the students retreat from the square. Inside the campus, funeral music was mixed with the sound of weeping. White flowers hung on the trees; teachers and students wore black arm bands; wreaths hung on the tops of gates. Before the campus's main building, there was a declaration calling for the resignation of Party members. Professors were searching for their students as department heads checked for missing students and teachers. Students were filling soda bottles with gasoline, preparing to resist the army's advance.

Around noon, two trucks filled with troops arrived. They claimed that they were from the 40th Army of the northeast, and said they would fight the evil 27th Army and

Changan Avenue.
Peter Charlesworth (JB Pictures)

One group approached the convoy and told the soldiers, "Get off. We're going to burn this truck." The soldiers obediently climbed down . . .

defend the university. The students thought about it, and finally decided not to accept the offer. In their hearts they wished that there were enough honest soldiers to declare war against the Fascist government. At 3:30 P.M., we heard two tear gas canisters explode outside our room. We thought the army had marched in to occupy the school, and nine of us huddled together inside the room, waiting for the soldiers' onslaught.

Throughout the night, sporadic gunshots could be heard. When day broke, however, the army still hadn't entered the school. It began occurring to students that they ought to flee; Molotov cocktails, black arm bands, loud-speakers, white flowers, and wreaths were cleared away. Students and teachers began to scrape away all the big-character posters, while others left school for home or the houses of relatives.

I met several students returning from collecting donations for the injured students. I told them that I would go to my dormitory to get some money for them. They said that I should take the money to the office of the Autonomous Student Union. When I got to the office ten minutes later, everyone had already left. Two bunk beds, several tables, some papers, and blankets were all that remained.

Everyone had already gone underground.

Fortunately, I had a return ticket to the United States, so I decided to hide at a friend's place for a few days.

H. and several of his friends also decided to flee Beijing. H.'s cousin was a standing committee member in the university's Student Union. He bore bruises from being clubbed the night before but stubbornly insisted on staying on campus. He had faced more danger than any of us. We finally convinced him to leave Beijing with H. as we helped him change his bloodstained clothes for fresh ones. I gave him the only ten U.S. dollars I had on me; it's easier to get a cab with foreign money.

"Hurry up, hurry up." That was our last farewell. We had been good friends for many years. None of us knew what awaited. "Brothers, when are we going to see each other again?" I thought. Through my tears, I watched them disappear into the crowd.

I started walking at a fast clip toward my friend's house. I looked for a taxi but couldn't find one. Suddenly, a van stopped in front of me. A middle-aged man stuck his head out of the window and asked, "Where are you going?"

"Anwai Xiaoguan," I replied in a hurry.

These images were made by Fang Mu, an amateur photographer who lives in Muxudi, an apartment complex overlooking Changan Avenue. In the first frame on the left, APCs smolder. Soldiers in the third frame watch as civilians board a seized APC.

At that moment, there was a call to "Shoot the choppers, shoot the choppers!" People looked everywhere for bullets; some suggested asking the soldiers . . .

"Give me twelve yuan," he demanded. I gave him the money.

"Are you one of the escaping students?"

"Yes," I said. I expected some sympathy and a fare reduction.

"I'm sorry, I can't take you," he said. "There are soldiers everywhere."

"Please help me," I begged.

"No, I'm here for business, and I can't afford to get into trouble."

I watched the van disappear, feeling lost.

"Brother, where are you going?" asked a man with a three-wheeled cart. He had an Anhui accent.

"Hop on. Six yuan."

I lay on the cart, staring at the blue sky while the cart rolled slowly along.

After a while a middle-aged man stopped us. With him were two young people who looked like students and looked as if they had barely made it out of the square in one piece.

"Could you take these two Nanjing University students to the railway station?" the man asked.

"How about ten?" the driver said.

"We are penniless," one of the students said pitifully. By now, six or seven people had gathered around us.

"Your damned heart is black," a young bystander said angrily. "They'll be caught if they don't get away. You want to make money from other people's misery?"

I jumped out of the cart and handed the driver ten yuan.

"Here's your money," I said. "Take them to the station."

"Don't give him a cent," the crowd shouted.

"Okay, okay, I won't take the money. I'll take them there," the cyclist said.

"Twenty yuan," the driver said. "Ten each."

The two students shook their heads.

"The students don't have money. Why do you ask for so much?" the man said angrily.

"Fifteen for two."

The two students still shook their heads.

The two students climbed on the cart and left.

"Are you also trying to get away?" someone asked me. I told him where I wanted to go.

"I live there, too. I'll take you," a young man said. I jumped on the back of his bicycle.

"Tell your classmates they are welcome to stay with us," the man said. "We can hide many of you."

My eyes grew wet and I was at a loss for words.

The airport was in chaos. Everyone was shoving and pushing, and struggling to get through with their luggage. Even foreigners forgot their manners and were pushing and yelling. I didn't see any armed police, and everyone was loudly swapping stories of what they had heard and seen.

When we got on the plane, my thoughts went back to the experiences of the past few days. It seemed like a nightmare or a movie saturated with violence in which I had played a part. When the plane took off, the foreigners applauded and cheered, but as the ground fell away and blurred, I wondered, "Did I just leave like this?" I saw in my mind my friend H., his cousin, the girl with the bloody face, and the person crushed by the tank. Tears streamed down my face. I took out the black arm band and put it on my left arm.

I thought of a song that someone had taught me a few days before.

> A stray bullet hit my chest;
> Suddenly the past swelled in my heart.
> I wept, but without sorrow.
> If this is the last shot,
> I will accept it as an honor.
> Oh, the last shot.
> There is so much to say.
> There is so much to enjoy.
> There are so many like myself,
> Victims of the last shot.
> Clinging to the warm earth,
> Sunrise and sunset;
> The flowers and trees blossom;
> I only have one thing to say:
> Don't let go.
>
> —*Yang Jianli*

At noon on June 4, I was two miles away, but I could already see thick black smoke billowing over Muxudi. By the time I got there, more than thirty armored vehicles had been burned. People were beginning to set fire to army trucks. One group approached the convoy and told the soldiers, "Get off. We're going to burn this truck." The soldiers obediently climbed down, bringing along whatever was on the truck. The people then poured gasoline on the canvas coverings and burned the vehicles.

Expressionless, all the soldiers sat on the curb and sidewalk, their guns piled next to them as they watched the fire. I walked over and told them what I had seen in Tiananmen Square; other people, with tears in their eyes or crying out loud, told them what had happened the night before. I asked the soldiers whether they knew what was going on in Beijing, and they said no. A soldier with a Shanxi* accent told me

---

* Shanxi is a province in North China, just west of Beijing.

Changan Avenue on June 4, as seen from the Beijing Hotel. Citizens scramble for cover.
Fred Scott

"I have to carry out my orders. . . . Otherwise, I'd be court-martialed. But let me tell you one thing: the ones who gave those orders are damned bastards!"

that it had been at least a week since their radios were confiscated, and they were forbidden to read any newspapers. Other soldiers nodded their heads to corroborate this.

I gave an officer a detailed description of what I had seen.

When I finished, he said, "Many of you have told me the same thing. But I'm a PLA man, and I have to carry out my orders, even orders that might result in what you saw. Otherwise, I'd be court-martialed. But let me tell you one thing: the ones who gave those orders are damned bastards!" He was very emotional when he said this, his voice trembling slightly. I could see the anger in his eyes.

All the while, army choppers flew back and forth overhead, repeatedly broadcasting this message: "Orders from the Military Committee: the troops must not be stopped. The troops must assault anyone who tries to block them."

Around 2:00 P.M., near the Muxudi Bridge, two of the thirty-odd armored vehicles had still not been burned. A man climbed into one and started it. People cheered because they now had a driver of their own. Others scrambled onto the armed personnel carrier to play around with its antiaircraft gun.

At this point, a rather tall man in his thirties dressed in civilian clothes urged them not to tamper with the military equipment. Some young men asked him who he was. He took out his work ID, which showed that he was a colonel at the Navy Hospital. By then, the people's hatred of soldiers was running very high, and some people, believing him to be a plainclothes policeman, started beating him. He tried to run away, but they chased him, throwing bricks. One brick cut his head and another one hit him on the back. He ran toward the military museum. Others were less sure about him being a spy and shouted, "Stop beating him!"

At that moment, a chopper flew overhead again, and there was a call to "Shoot the choppers, shoot the choppers!" People looked everywhere for bullets; some suggested asking the soldiers for ammunition.

Shortly thereafter, a soldier brought a whole case of bullets from one of the trucks, and a crowd tried to load the antiaircraft gun on the armored vehicle. About twenty minutes later, they were able to shoot off a round. The gunshots were so loud they hurt my ears even though I had covered them. I took a look at the people who had fired the guns and wondered how they could stand the deafening noise. I saw them wrap their T-shirts around their heads and shoot randomly at the sky. After shooting off two rounds they stopped and received a loud round of applause. The soldiers were still not responding. The vehicle then drove toward People's University.

—*Gao Huan, a student from Qinghua University*

Around noon on June 4, I arrived at the flat of Professors Fang Lizhi and Li Shuxian, who were nearly trembling. They just kept saying, "It's extremely dangerous! . . . they've gone mad!" When I left them to go home for lunch, Professor Li said that if she called and said, "Bring your children over to play," it would mean they were in trouble.

About 5:00 P.M., she called and invited my children over. I found a taxi and went. At that point, they wanted to go to a tourist hotel where the presence of foreigners and journalists might make an arrest more difficult, and in any case would make it immediately obvious to the world if it did happen. Professor Fang suggested the Jianguo Hotel, noting its proximity to the United States embassy. I suggested the nearer Shangri-La Hotel, mainly because there were reports of continued shooting in the city, and the forty-five-minute ride across town, as dusk was falling, did not seem wise to me. Moreover, I knew that an American news crew was still renting a floor at the Shangri-La Hotel. The Fangs agreed. At the Shangri-La, I extracted a promise of strict confidence from the news crew; I left the Fangs in a comfortable room and went home.

I returned the next morning and found that the Fangs had not left their room at all. I got them some orange juice and croissants, and then asked what they wanted to do. Professor Li telephoned one of her students at Beijing University to ask how things looked there. During the conversation she became more and more upset, until she could barely maintain her composure. She told us that the students were expecting the army to take over their campus that night; they were stockpiling bricks and bottles with which to resist the tanks—knowing full well that this would, in all likelihood, cost them their lives. Professor Li said that her students hoped, above all else, that she and Professor Fang would remain safe and continue to speak out for democracy in China. Then their deaths would "have meaning." Professor Fang turned to me and said, "Let's not go to lunch. Let's go to the embassy."

I checked with the news crew to see if the streets to the embassy seemed passable. What worried me most was whether we would be tailed and then "diverted" by the police, and then, if we got to the embassy gate, how I would get the Fangs past the PLA guards who were stationed there. There seemed little I could do about the first problem, but to help with the second I asked a young American who was with the news crew to accompany us so that he could remain in the car with the Fangs while I got out with my passport to get the gate open. Then, I thought, they could all hurry through the gate as I held it open.

The ride was extremely nerve-racking but uneventful save for one unforeseen citizens' roadblock, which our driver

A series by Magnum photographer Stuart Franklin.
A worker pauses in the middle of Changan
Avenue, as tanks roll out of the square . . .

The tanks approach . . .

figured out how to get around. At the gate of the embassy, my plan for getting in worked just as I had hoped. There were two army guards there, but they seemed not to recognize Fang.

Inside, we went first to the office of an official in the Press and Cultural Section. Later we were joined by a political officer. We had crackers and peanut butter as a makeshift lunch.

Then began a long afternoon of talk about what to do. The first interruption, chillingly, was a volley of rifle and automatic-weapons fire from troops who were parading up the street directly outside the window of the office where we were sitting. Professor Fang said he hoped his family might stay a few days in the embassy until the situation became clearer. He also hoped this could be done without publicity or notification of the Chinese government.

The embassy officials quickly pointed out that secrecy was impossible, that the Chinese staff at the embassy must have already noticed Fang's entry, and that hidden microphones were presumably already at work. They explained

that "political asylum" was not an alternative, because this could be granted only to persons who were already in America. The alternative that could be considered, they said, was called "temporary refuge." If granted, the Fangs (who had arrived with only two small air-travel bags) would have to face the possibility of indefinite confinement to a very small place. Professor Fang agreed with the officials that the Chinese government's response would most likely be to denounce the United States for harboring him, to denounce him for seeking protection, and to vilify the whole Chinese democracy movement by saying it was plotted and backed by foreign forces. All these points weighed against "temporary refuge."

For a time, the question remained one of whether there couldn't be some middle ground between a formal request for refuge, and the truly frightening prospect of simply walking back out onto the street. Professor Fang told me he thought they should not ask for refuge, even if their lives were in danger. He said he thought the Chinese government would try to incriminate the democracy movement, and he

And a confrontation develops . . .

wanted to do what was best for the cause. Professor Li said nothing, although she continued to seem somewhat more upset than Professor Fang.

As we left the embassy and headed for the Jianguo Hotel, Professor Fang commented that "I think it would be good if the American Embassy gave protection to some ordinary people—a worker, a student, or just a regular townsperson like the ones who were killed last night. It would be a good statement about human rights—much better than taking in a famous person."

At the hotel, we tried to avoid people, who began recognizing Fang, and sat in a far corner of the Cantonese restaurant. After dinner, I brought the Fang family to Room 400, which had been rented by a friend of mine. He was about to leave for Shanghai and agreed to let the Fangs stay in his room. I myself was eager to get back across town to my family before dark, and left the Fangs shortly after 7:00 P.M. That was the last time I spoke with them.

—*Perry Link*

At 11:00 P.M. on June 6, I left my house on my bicycle. I wanted to see what the troops were doing. Riding along the Second Ring Road, I passed over Fuchengmen Bridge and followed the route of the number 102 bus to Xidan. I was very cautious the whole way. When I got to Fuchengmen I asked a bystander, "Is anything going on up ahead?" If not, I would continue on. He said it was clear.

I passed Baitasi and Xisi, and finally arrived at the vicinity of Xidan and the Nationalities Palace. I heard the sound of cannon fire from Liuliqiao. I was on the north side of Changan Avenue. A man was squatting by the side of the road, smoking a cigarette, next to a young couple talking. I was behind him, about two or three steps away.

In an alley off to the side about forty young citizens were loudly cursing the troops. As they cursed the troops they heard the roar of tanks coming and began to run away. Then they heard the tanks stop. They resumed their cursing, and the troops opened fire in their direction, blasting leaves and branches off the elm trees around us.

We thought it was very funny at the time. We just

A dialogue begins . . .

wanted to curse the soldiers and hear them fire their guns. Since they were far away from us, they couldn't see us. But after one round of firing, the guy squatting on the side of the road suddenly lost his balance. At first, the young couple near him didn't notice. But when they saw that he wasn't talking, they nudged him and found that he had been shot and was covered with blood.

He groaned when people stretched him out flat to carry him to the hospital, but then he didn't make another sound.

—*Huang Yan, a student at Beijing Normal University*

From *The People's Daily*, June 11, 1989, "A Sunday Street Scene in Beijing"

Today, the first Sunday since the suppression of the counter-revolutionary rebellion, was calm and peaceful in the capital. In Wangfujing, Xidan, Dongsi, and other busy commercial districts, large and small stores were open for business. Although few people went shopping during this past week, today *there were a lot of customers. The vegetable markets and food stores were bustling. Fresh cucumbers, tender kidney beans, shiny eggplant, ripe red tomatoes, and other seasonal vegetables filled the racks.*

The private vendors, who stayed at home the past few days, have once again appeared on the streets in large numbers. In the residential areas, one can occasionally hear the calls of the scrap collectors and smell the fragrant aroma of roasting lamb shish kebabs.

During the past week the atmosphere of the park on Dongdaqiao Road was cold and somber, but today it was back to normal. Old retired workers, in groups of three and four, played cards and chess. Some young people sat in the shade, kissing. A baby-sitter was looking after a few children who were playing on the swings.

On the main streets, when armed soldiers walked by, people no longer had frightened expressions. In spite of their exhaustion, martial law troops vigilantly patrolled the areas of the capital that they had been assigned to defend.

Since the transportation system is now running normally, postal workers are delivering letters again, and sanitation

Then abruptly ends, as the
tanks resume their progress.

That's strategy! You will never win a war using pen and mouth while your enemy uses bullets. Do you agree?

workers are taking away the trash. The rate of attendance at factories is rising every day, and the Bureau of Education has already notified all the primary and middle schools that they must return to their normal class schedule by June 12.

Airplanes and trains have been running on normal schedules the past few days. A passenger from Tianjin told this reporter that he had heard a lot of rumors about Beijing while he was in Tianjin, so he was a little nervous about coming. But after he left the station, took a look around, and saw that everything was just the same as it was before, he felt much more at ease.

A telephone interview with Dai Qing

Q: Why did you withdraw from the Communist party? What influence do you think it will have?

A: This was a personal action; I do not think it will cause a movement or attract any attention. I only wanted to get away from politics. I don't wish to participate in any more political activities, and I withdrew from the Party to complete my personal development. Withdrawing from it does not imply that I oppose it; I still wish the Party well.

Q: What was your immediate reason for leaving the Party? Has the Party responded to you?

A: I withdrew on the fourth of June. I cannot accept the tragedy which I witnessed on June 3 and 4. They may ask me why, but up to today, they have not done so.

Q: How have you felt since you left the Party?

A: I foresaw all of these events. I warned them, but no one would listen to me.

Q: Won't withdrawing from the Party affect your work and your life?

A: I just want to be a law-abiding citizen. Perhaps, as a non-Party member, my journalistic activity will be restricted.

Q: It is said there have been more than 400 a[rrested]
so-called counterrevolutionaries who were [...in]
the "turmoil."

A: Up to now, the government's target for pu[nishment]
has been the rioters. I have not seen inte[llectuals]
arrested for having expressed their personal opinions.
Whether this will change, I do not know.

Q: Isn't it true that intellectuals have now practically
stopped contacting each other?

A: Everyone suspects that his telephone has been tapped.
So they rarely contact each other. On the other
hand, in the current situation, the intellectuals have
nothing to do, and it is inappropriate to participate
in any organized activities.

Q: In your opinion, how did the national situation turn
into such a mess?

A: I do not think that Deng Xiaoping and Li Peng
intended to make such a mess of our country;
neither did the students. The problem was that both
sides always insisted on having their own way;
neither ever listened to the other or considered the
other's opinion. I believe that the goals of the two
sides were rather close, but the paths they chose
were too far apart. Therefore, it finally became a
life-and-death struggle. This is also why I decided to
stay far away from politics, which saddens me. Why
couldn't they have been more tolerant of each other?
At the end, the students claimed to overthrow the
government, but what would they do after they had
done so? Who had the ability to take over?

From the government's perspective, all this was
extremely counterrevolutionary. It was unforgiveable.
There was no possible compromise. Therefore, the
situation was pushed to the extreme. This kind of
political struggle is too primitive.

Alon Reininger (Contact Press Images)

A PLA soldier. The characters on the bus
read, "He killed four people."
Zong Hoi Yi (VU)

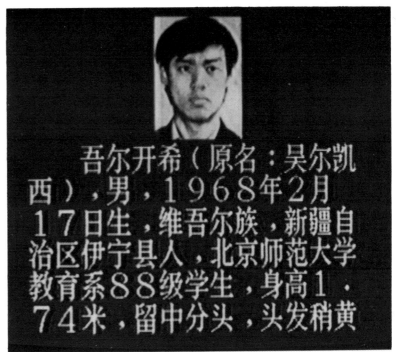

All-points bulletin for Wuer Kaixi on Chinese television.   *Abbas (Magnum)*

Q: After this catastrophe, when do you think the situation will recover?

A: This must wait until the old-generation politicians pass from the scene. As long as they're still here, there is no hope for change. Nevertheless, this is still a little better than having the whole country in turmoil. Carrying out martial law was seen as a means to prevent even greater chaos, and I know that, from now on, the generals will begin to develop their own bases of power. If Deng Xiaoping cannot control the situation, then the generals will become warlords.

Q: Sooner or later Deng will pass away. Do you think there will be regional warlordism after his death?

A: That depends on how the reform goes. You cannot always let the guns do the talking. The whole world is now entering an era of détente rather than relying on military force. How can China still have a civilization if we only rely on guns? What can the intellectuals hope for?

Q: Do you have the feeling that you are personally in danger, especially since June 4?

A: I have always felt very calm. I never participated in any of the events which were considered by the government as part of the turmoil. Since the end of April, I tried to persuade everyone not to escalate the dangerous situation. If they're still going to persecute me, what can I do? The people who fled did so either because they were afraid or because they knew that they had violated martial law.

Q: How would you view the Tiananmen massacre?

A: Up to June 2, I still supported martial law because I believed that Tiananmen Square needed to be brought under control. But I never thought they

Mid-June, massive arrests begin. Reports said that 10,000 to 30,000 citizens were detained.
Manuel Vimenet (VU)

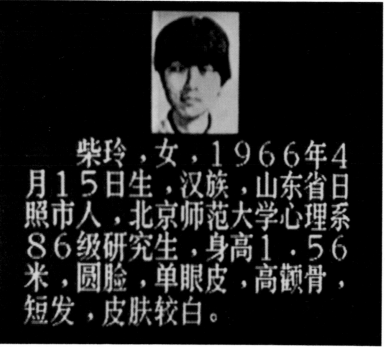

柴玲，女，１９６６年４
月１５日生，汉族，山东省日
照市人，北京师范大学心理系
８６级研究生，身高１．５６
米，圆脸，单眼皮，高颧骨，
短发，皮肤较白。

Portrait and description of Chai Ling.   *Abbas (Magnum)*

would do it this way. They destroyed the best of the
new generation. That is too great a sacrifice.

Q: In this atmosphere, isn't it true that the government
and the people are already standing on opposite
sides? How can this standoff be resolved?

A: It's too difficult. The government should not have
done what it did.

In order to stop the student movement and the turmoil,
the Party and the government have exhibited a great deal of
control and restraint. We have done more than any other
government in the world would have done, and many members of the international media agree. Comrade Li Peng and
myself, and many other leaders, have conducted extensive
dialogue with the students. . . .

I understand how you young people feel. You took to
the streets, demanding more democracy and reforms against
corruption. Your intentions were good. But now, when the
evidence shows clearly that the student movement evolved
into a counterrevolutionary rebellion, some young people
still cannot accept the truth. So, organizing self-reflection
and self-education has become a very demanding task.

—*Yuan Mu, official spokesman of the State Council*

**A letter from a Chinese professor to an
American colleague who taught in Beijing.**

Beijing, June 14, 1989

Dear Kyle,

*How are you? Professor Liu already gave me your re-
gards. Thank you. I'm very relieved to know that you returned
home safely.*

Broadcast of an interrogation.
Abbas (Magnum)

Everyone from Building Number 8 has left. Only a few custodians remain. After you went, I took care of all your stuff. Those two little rugs you had—I gave them to my cats.

Please send me some American stamps so I can give letters to my American friends to mail in the United States. From now on, we cannot write you directly anymore. Every letter has to be brought out by someone. I will enclose some Chinese stamps so if there's someone coming to China, you can ask him to mail it in Beijing. They even check my letters to relatives elsewhere in China. We're not supposed to say anything about what happened here.

There are still a few students left, so we're still teaching. The student public address system is gone, and so are all the big-character posters. No crowds gather on the streets anymore. But inside the offices people are still talking. The people of Beijing are very brave. They're not afraid. Since the night of June 8, soldiers have been patrolling every intersection, checking identification. Small skirmishes are still taking place. More than 500 people have been arrested. Yesterday they began to broadcast the names of the most-wanted student leaders—there are twenty-one in all. Wang Dan and Wuer Kaixi are among them.

Two people from our school have been arrested. One is a teacher from our department who made speeches at the square. The other one is a worker. We don't know what they're going to do to them. I am prepared. I'm not afraid.

I imagine that you must have seen Western news coverage of what happened on June 3 and 4. What was it really like? How many really died? Who knows?

In China, if you don't know anything at all, you may be able to live happily. But the more you know, the more pain you must feel. We are suffocating here. As I write to you now, I want to cry. Since the massacre, it has been either cloudy or rainy every day in Beijing. It seems to me that even the heavens are saddened.

When the summer vacation starts, if I still haven't been arrested, I will clean all your clothes and put them in the suitcase. There are still many things you liked and needed in your room. I will take care of them. I've put aside the small things you need, such as makeup, and your daughter's toys.

When you write to me, please never write in English on the envelope. It's better to make your own envelopes out of white paper instead of using American ones.

Wish happiness to your family and all your friends.

A letter from a student in the Provinces to his American teacher

Beijing, June 14, 1989

Dear Sarah:

There is so much to say that I don't know where to begin.

School ended on July 5, and we spent the following three days buried in the terrible "study" of the documents from the

Cleaning up debris on Changan Avenue.

Central Government. We had to study almost seven hours each day. After studying, our political consciousness "improved" a lot. We now know that our "childish" enthusiasm was exploited by a small handful of people. Fortunately, these people have been discovered by our great leader Comrade Little Bottle* and have been quelled by the people's democratic dictatorship. We also know that our Party is the strongest party in the world; it will never lose because it has a pair of iron hands. Our PLA men love the people so deeply that 6,000 fully armed soldiers were killed and hurt by the people's bare hands, while only 300 students and bystanders were killed by mistake.

What a story! But I had to believe it completely in my "reflection" (a current form of self-criticism, in which you must tell the government how you behaved in this movement and the lessons you've learned after the three-day study; you also express your attitude toward the Party, the leaders, and socialism). In my reflection, I regretted, regretted, and regret-

---

* This is a play on Deng Xiaoping's name. *Xiao ping* means little bottle.

night, I would awaken, terrified that it was after us. It was impossible to stay in any one place too long because the friends who were hiding us would become very nervous, so we moved around from village to village.

At one point, I was offered a job as a watchman at a rarely visited warehouse. But I didn't accept the offer, because I thought I would be unconvincing as a watchman—I looked too intellectual.

We thought of hiding in the mountains, but there was no food being shipped there, and we had no tents to protect us from wild animals and insects. We even thought of buying bikes and traveling to Shanxi, Yunnan, or Guizhou, but we decided to leave China instead.

It was extremely dangerous when my wife and I were escaping. If we hadn't made it out of China, I would have had a nervous breakdown. I am not able to disclose how we finally escaped from China.

—Yan Jiaqi

ted; flattered, flattered, and flattered. I know I shouldn't have been so hypocritical, but I had to protect myself; we have to protect ourselves. Not only do our parents want us to do so, but history and the future of our motherland require us to do so.

That's strategy! You will never win a war using pen and mouth while your enemy uses bullets. Do you agree?

I heard it through the grapevine that Wang Dan has been arrested in Nanjing. I hope it is not true.

I was hiding in the countryside. At first, I didn't want to leave Beijing. I thought that the worst that could happen was that I would be jailed for a year, and then, upon my release, my reputation would be restored. When the official order to arrest me was issued, I changed my mind and decided to run for my life.

I stayed about fifteen days in the countryside. I discovered that the dictatorship of the Chinese government had seeped through every corner of Chinese society. During the day we were not able to go out. Whenever a car passed at

REFLECTIONS...

AND EPILOGUE

Chinese culture is basically a feudalistic and despotic one that totally negates the individual; yet it has endured for 5,000 years. That culture is based on a set of rigidly defined relationships—between the emperor and his officials, husband and wife, father and son, and so forth. But it clearly provides no rights, of any kind, for ordinary people.

This feudalistic culture was brought to a climax by Mao Zedong after 1949. But further distortion of human nature by the Cultural Revolution gave rise to tremendous popular resistance. Then, with the policies of reform and the "open door" promoted by Comrade Deng Xiaoping, long-repressed individuality went off in the opposite direction, in a blind pursuit of the self.

Individualism was a powerful trend among the present generation even before the 1989 pro-democracy movement. College students began rebelling against all kinds of authority—at times it seemed their favorite word was "No!" Another phenomenon that you might find strange is that some students stood naked on the roofs of buildings and screamed, "I am what I am!" Such incidents were vivid proof that Chinese youth had developed a powerful sense of self as well as a profound idealism.

All this, however, was totally at odds with the nature of our present society. Because of the contradictions between our new idealism and China's feudalistic reality, my generation felt completely lost.

The most influential people among us were not Fang Lizhi or Wei Jingsheng, but Cui Jian, the famous pop singer, the poet Bei Dao, the Taiwanese singer Qi Qin, and poets like Gu Cheng and others. For example, the popularity of Cui Jian's song "I Have Absolutely Nothing" suggests some of our disorientation.

This sense is also manifested in the emergence of a large number of campus poets. The most famous was a fellow leader of the democracy movement, Wang Dan. Sometimes I write poems, too. One of my poems is called "Rain."

> I pour my heart out to the white cloud,
> I, the homesick wanderer.
> Oh, please, float back to my native land,
> And drop the tears I shed for my mother.

I wrote this poem three years ago. At the time, I never thought it would mean as much as it does today.

There is a song written by Qi Qin, which, even during the hunger strike in Tiananmen Square, you could hear being played on every cassette player.

> I'm a wolf from the north,
> Wandering in this boundless desolate land.

> The bitter north wind
> Is blowing up a storm of yellow sand.
> I clamp my frozen teeth,
> And give a howl or two,
> For no reason,
> Other than my longing for the beautiful prairie in that
>   legendary land.

I like to cite this song to illustrate my point about the disaffection of Chinese youth. This was the state of mind of Chinese young people before the 1989 pro-democracy movement.

—*Wuer Kaixi*

The student movement of 1989 had its roots in the earlier movement of 1986–87. The latter had little understanding of democracy and suffered a total defeat. While the movement of 1989 also failed, it demonstrated a far greater grasp of democratic theory and practice. Associations like Wang Dan's Democracy Salon, for instance, initiated serious discussions of democracy, while students gained some experience in the democratic process. They learned that democracy is not merely an idea; it is also an institution. It is not only the expression of differing views but also a compromise among those views.

We knew that we were making history, but we were also divided. The reformers within the Party, the Socialist democrats, students, and workers remained fundamentally separate. Only after getting to know some of the leaders of the workers during the student movement did I realize that a large number of workers' societies and organizations had been quite active in the past few years. If we had coordinated our efforts better, the movement might not have failed so tragically. In addition, the student movement lacked adequate organization and reformulated its plans unnecessarily; we were incapable of putting up an effective resistance when we were confronted with serious opposition.

A truly democratic political movement requires the participation of diverse forces. Solidarity in Poland succeeded because it collaborated with both the intellectuals and the church. But the Chinese intellectuals joined the student movement late and played only a supporting role. We were not prepared with practical tactics to back up democracy. Although everyone's goal in the recent movement was democracy, the workers' motives in joining the movement were different from ours. Some workers even carried placards that said, "Deng Xiaoping said that the intellectuals are number one; then where are we workers to be?" The intellectuals never sought to establish ideological, emotional, or personal relations with the workers.

Although we may have had a deeper understanding of democracy in 1989, we had not seriously thought out the

June 5. As rumors of an attack from opposition military units spread, PLA tanks took up positions at key intersections.
Liu Heung Shing (AP)

Before 1989, college students began rebelling against all kinds of authority. . . . Students stood naked on the roofs of buildings and screamed, "I am what I am!"

future development of democracy in China. As the situation rapidly changed, our theoretical shortcomings became more pronounced. We never practiced political rationality or made it the guiding principle of the student movement. In retrospect, if the movement had stopped after the May 4 rally or the hunger strike, it would have been a great victory. That would have been the rational thing to do.

But if a spontaneous mass movement is to behave rationally, its opponents must be rational as well. It was the irrationality of the government that inspired the irrationality of the movement. We repeatedly communicated to the senior levels of the government that if they wanted the students to withdraw, they had to "give them a ladder to climb down," so to speak, or else they would not go.

But the government consistently made the wrong decisions. At the beginning, we thought that the government was just stupid; in fact, Li Peng and the other elders had a premeditated plan. They were plotting to oust Zhao Ziyang and undo a decade of reforms. As the government continued to provoke the students, it therefore became more and more difficult to ask the young people to behave rationally.

Before the movement began, so many of these young people seemed hopelessly preoccupied either with entertaining themselves or with preparing for the TOEFL* exams. So many of them had been left disillusioned by politics after the suppression of the 1986–87 student movement. But the movement of 1989 made them see themselves differently. At last their individualism was allowed to develop fully, and with it an intense idealism that, once sparked, would blossom beautifully.

—Su Wei

The biggest mistake made by the democracy movement was that it failed to stop at the most advantageous point. When the movement was at its peak and the authorities began to show signs of giving in, people failed to make the compromises necessary to solidify their gains. Instead, they became overconfident, constantly making more demands, which, eventually, wore them down. Facing escalating demands, the authorities adopted a harder line, finally resorting to force.

At that stage, the democracy forces were too weak to fight a final decisive battle. In addition, the democracy forces never consolidated their gains and thus never had a solid base. Facing the bloody crackdown, they lost not only what they had won at the movement's peak but also the progress they had made before the movement.

---

*An acronym for the standardized test of English as a foreign language, TOEFL is a prerequisite for admission to an American university.

Some have argued that since the government did not compromise, the students should not contemplate compromise either. But that does not accurately reflect the government's position. While the government never openly retracted the harsh April 26 editorial, it did tone down the rhetoric; it even withdrew the accusation that the student movement had caused social turmoil. This softening of the official line, from critical editorials calling for a ban on the movement to simply ignoring the students, represented a compromise on the part of the government. This was a historic victory.

It is now clear that if the movement had wound down after the dialogue with Yan Mingfu on May 16, or after Zhao Ziyang's May 18 speech, it would have given the liberals in the government the upper hand. Further reforms would have been possible. The democracy forces would also have gained confidence and additional support and sympathy from the people, thus strengthening their efforts.

Why, then, did the movement keep going?

Mainly because the movement lacked effective leadership. It is true that organizations and influential leaders emerged from the movement. But the organizations could not discipline their members, and the leaders failed to lead their followers. Within each organization, everything was decided by vote, and no one assumed responsibility for the decisions. Anyone had the right to rebel, and no one had the obligation to comply. This was a misinterpretation of democracy.

Many Chinese are accustomed to listening to two types of leaders: those with charisma and those with real power. The first type usually go against the establishment. The second type usually oppose the sharing of power. The students were trying to establish a democratic movement, but they were not accustomed to paying attention to leaders who had been selected through a systematic process.

Furthermore, the leaders of the democracy movement suffered from two major shortcomings. Many of them preferred to follow the crowd, or even be pushed by the crowd; they never relied on their own opinions to persuade others. In addition, many of these leaders were dissidents rather than politicians. They had incredible courage and high moral standards, and were very brave and outspoken, especially under pressure, but they were not experienced in finding allies or compromising. They had a very strong spirit of self-sacrifice, but they lacked the common sense needed in political struggles.

The spectacular pro-democracy movement in 1989 showed eloquently that the Chinese people will pursue democracy and freedom with compassion and self-sacrifice. Its failure indicates that we still lack wisdom, strategies, and

If the students (were) to withdraw, the government had to "give them a ladder to climb down." But the government consistently made the wrong decisions.

techniques in political struggles. This is the most important lesson we can draw from this movement.

—*Hu Ping, leader of the 1980 Chinese student movement*

The most important lesson we learned from the democracy movement is that it is impossible to initiate political change solely within the framework of the Communist system—a system that is racked by fraud, corruption, and weakness. While our economic system is unstable, at least some aspects of it are detached from the political arena. Because of that, we were able to achieve some positive results through economic reform. To accomplish political reform, however, the foundations of the entire system must be altered. That reform must be accomplished at least partially by political forces outside the framework of the Party. That fact was not clear before the democracy movement; until then, many people still had the illusion that reform could take place within the existing system.

The continuous development of the democracy movement should be supported by economic development. The formation of a democratic system and society in China depends on the emergence and growth of the middle class.

It was no accident that privately owned enterprises enthusiastically supported the democracy movement. Confusion over property rights and economic development had generated widespread corruption, inflation, and unequal distribution—problems that urgently demanded resolution.

The failure of this movement was also inevitable, in part, because the Chinese entrepreneurial middle class was still so frail and small and lacked political representation.

If an independent political force does not form outside of the Communist party, the Party simply will not be able to continue reforms of any kind.

Can the system change itself? A barber cannot cut his own hair. The head of the Communist party also needs someone to prune its shaggy locks. That barber is the FDC.* The events of June 4 made it clear that a Communist party dictatorship inevitably leads to corruption and despotic rule. The sole dictatorship of the Communist party has now ended. The Chinese people have lost hope completely, but in hopelessness lies the seed of new hope.

—*Wan Runnan, former chairman, Stone Computer Corp.*

A planned economy needs an authoritarian government in order to enforce its plans, while a free economy requires a democratic system to safeguard it. Our economic reforms called for a redistribution of resources, our political reforms for a redistribution of power.

Zhao Ziyang believed that the problems that China currently faces are due to a failure to complete the reforms; the conservatives, on the other hand, believed that the problems were caused by the reforms themselves.

Since the majority of first-generation leaders were peasant revolutionaries, they were unaccustomed to both the market economy and democratic politics. The second-generation leaders were brought up during the period of constant class struggle, and when they heard differing opinions, they were only capable of thinking of it as another stage of class struggle.

Several old Party leaders had so completely manipulated the Politburo that Zhao Ziyang and the reformers were reduced to a minority within the government. By the end of 1988, the economic, political, and social problems had festered into a disaster just waiting to happen. Zhao Ziyang understood that he might be forced out at any time.

There was still a balance of power, however, between the weak reformers and the strong conservatives because of the many positive and obvious changes that reforms had brought to the country. Farmers' income had increased by 260 percent, while city dwellers' income increased by about 70 percent. People in general had become more outspoken; the market was livelier. People generally agreed that flawed reforms were better than no reforms at all. The conservatives hadn't yet found a good excuse to get rid of the reformers. The democracy movement of 1989 provided the opportunity they had been looking for.

The June massacre was a well-orchestrated coup against the decade of reform. If the students had been more strategically mature, would there have been a massacre? Yes. No matter when the students withdrew, Li Peng would have done something to provoke them. For example, after Zhao spoke on May 4, the students were ready to return to their universities. But on May 6, Li called in the presidents of six major universities in Beijing and told them, "Zhao's speech represents only his own opinion. The April 26 editorial represents the position of the Party and Deng Xiaoping." It was this that inspired the students to resort to the hunger strike. On April 24, Bao Tong was excluded from the Politburo meeting. On May 15, I learned that my own name was on the conservatives' blacklist. The government claimed that the students were carrying out a "conspiracy." But it is clear where the real conspiracy lay.

—*Chen Yizi*

---

* The FDC (Federation for a Democratic China) was headed by Yan Jiaqi, Wan Runnan, and Wuer Kaixi and is based in Paris.

Deng Xiaoping regards the massacre at Tiananmen Square as a great victory because hundreds of thousands of dissident students and their supporters were brought under control, and order has been restored to the streets of Beijing. The truth, of course, is that the uprising was the greatest show of democratic force in over forty years of Communist rule in China. It gave the Chinese people confidence in their strength and exposed the deep rifts with the Party leadership. The movement ended with the old ruling clique returning to the old political system, but its grip on the country is more feeble than ever. The extraordinary power and potential of China's democracy movement is now clear.

In sharp contrast are the isolation, weakness, hypocrisy, and brutality of the Communist rulers. Two general secretaries of the Party have been dismissed within two and a half years. And it was only by forcing every provincial Party committee to declare its support for the dismissal of Zhao Ziyang and the appointment of Jiang Zeming that the top central leaders were able to gain the formal majority necessary to pass this measure. These leaders themselves are largely controlled by eight senile "retired emperors," all over eighty years old, who do not hold formal office in the Party or government but who prop up their rule through brute force and lies. Deng and his cohorts have lost the confidence of the Chinese people and thus the legitimate right to rule.

To Deng, as to Mao, people are nothing more than instruments: in wartime they serve as soldiers; in peacetime they are hands for production. Despite his supreme position Deng, of course, did not act alone. Those who have significant influence over him include Party elders Chen Yun and Bo Yibo, who have made every effort to derail economic reform; Hu Qiaomu and Deng Liqun, who stubbornly uphold Maoist ideology; Peng Zhen and Li Xiannian, who favor "old people's politics" and refuse to retire; and Wang Zhen and Yang Shangkun, who cling to a superstitious belief in military force. It was inevitable that Deng would be influenced by this faction. Having spent much of his life in the military, he too has an almost mystical confidence in the power of the military. With the help of these ossified ideologues, he destroyed the reform project that he created. They all refuse to see that the political system is destroying itself from within.

—Liu Binyan, a Chinese journalist and an outspoken critic of Party corruption

Some people say that if the students had evacuated the square earlier, then there wouldn't have been a massacre. But this wasn't likely.

The lesson we must draw from this bloody event is that political reform is absolutely essential in China. Deng Xiaoping has always said that he wants to "safeguard" the People's Republic, but it is a "people's" republic in name only. The Party has completely lost the confidence of the people because it has committed so many mistakes and crimes, like the Anti-Rightist movement in 1957, the Cultural Revolution —and the June 4 massacre. Political reform cannot come from the Communist party. If the FDC does not do this work now, somebody else will do it later. We are part of an irreversible trend.

The first step for the FDC is to legitimize itself. This is an arduous task. Its priorities are to develop its organization and to contact all of the intellectuals and overseas Chinese, whose support is particularly important for our legitimacy. The FDC should carry on publicity work, commenting on political issues concerning the Chinese government. Another priority is to make the organization legal inside China, to develop democratic legislation, and to revise the constitution.

The FDC should aim at incorporating workers, farmers, and intellectuals into the movement. Most of the people who actually blocked the tanks were not students but factory workers. Students took the lead and intellectuals participated actively, but the workers were the main force; they have a deep hatred for rule by dictatorship.

Although the farmers did not participate in the movement, they want democracy, too. They want to choose who is suitable to be the head of their villages, and the head of their country. With the development of privately owned farms, farmers have developed a real sense of democracy, as we discovered when we went to the countryside. They want to exercise their rights.

The day will come when Li Peng steps down. At that time, the constitution will be rewritten and the democracy movement of 1989 will be vindicated. The FDC could well become an opposition party within a democratic framework. The Communist party has a right to co-exist with the other parties; we do not want to overthrow the Communists, but people should have the right to make a choice. Only through the democratic process can we genuinely rebuild the republic. Governmental power must be divided between the legislative, executive, and judicial branches in order to break up the central power system that is traditional in China.

People must have the right to elect and to criticize their government. Leaders like Deng should never be allowed to suppress the will of the people or impose themselves on the people in the name of the Party or of socialism. People must be able to depose such leaders through legitimate means. We don't deny that there may be more bloodshed and sacrifice. However, we should still hold high the banner of peace, nonviolence, and reason in our effort to achieve the kind of nation we wish. In time, China will become a democracy.

—Yan Jiaqi

A demonstrator is detained by police.
Abbas (Magnum)

During the tense week
after the crackdown.
Peter Charlesworth (JB Pictures)

EPILOGUE

by Andrew J. Nathan

n the epilogue to *War and Peace,* Tolstoy writes, "The movement of peoples is not produced by the exercise of power; nor by intellectual activity, nor even by a combination of the two, as historians have supposed; but by the activity of *all* the men taking part in the event, who are always combined in such a way that those who take the most direct part in the action take the smallest share in the responsibility for it, and *vice versa.*" So, too, in Tiananmen, the acts of millions of ordinary people, not the will of great men, made history.

Children of the Dragon records these acts. People come to the square with children. They wear holiday clothes, eat ice cream sticks, take photographs, play guitars. They raise their fingers in a victory sign. Art students assemble a plaster statue of liberty, surrounded by red, blue, white, and yellow silk flags.

Students march toward the center of Beijing and meet a line of police; the police strike out and some marchers hit back. A student leader is lifted off his feet and carried forward by the crowd. Intellectuals trying to persuade demonstrators to withdraw from a government office find themselves at the head of a procession. One says, "We are completely powerless and are being pushed into the streets by the course of events." Students look forward to being heroes; they ask a teacher who lived through the cultural revolution what it is like to be in jail.

Individual decisions converge on consequences no one wants. A citizen finds himself being shot at; a soldier finds himself shooting. The bullets are real. A man touches his shirt and feels it soaked with blood.

Tragedy, Aristotle said, involves acts "which occur unexpectedly, and at the same time in consequence of one another." Forty years ago, the Chinese leaders set out to create a popular government that could mobilize all the country's resources for industrialization. They built a system that tied the peasants to the land, kept consumption to a minimum, fixed each person permanently in place in a work unit dominated by a single party secretary against whom there was no appeal, classified each individual as a member of a good or bad class, and called on each citizen to show that he or she was progressive by demonstrating enthusiasm for disciplining himself and persecuting others. Mao's people complied out of patriotism, a sense of unworthiness, faith in a despot's wisdom, and because they preferred to be among the victimizers than among the victims.

But one by one, people began to ask questions when they were denounced and jailed, or forced to go to the countryside to "learn from the peasants," only to find the villages dirty and destitute, or when they realized that Lin Biao, Mao's chosen successor, was a traitor.

The Chinese stopped believing that their poverty and suffering were redeemed by a greater purpose. Citizens demanded reparation of injuries and injustices done over the course of thirty years; millions applied for redress. A new generation wanted possessions, pleasure, and freedom. They would not "petition on their knees."

A dictator rules by recruiting his people to oppress one another. Mao's successors could no longer win people's cooperation by promising a future utopia. They had to produce or get out of the way. As people's lives improved, they got angrier. They had more to eat and wear but less than they felt they deserved; more living space but too little for comfort. Prices went up faster than wages. A few entrepreneurs and party officials lived in comfort, seemingly with unfair gains. A thin prosperity mocked years of sacrifice.

Reform made life better for most Chinese, but it also weakened the instruments of control. It dissolved the system of class labels that set citizen against citizen, restored educated people to authority, removed the rationale for political campaigns, and weakened the powers of the unit by giving people alternatives. People could move around the country, talk, think, and even write more freely.

The loosening of repression allowed people to reflect on what they had done, what they had seen others do, and what they had tolerated being done. Life during the past thirty years was a theme that dominated fiction, poetry, memoirs, biographies, histories, and philosophical works. Writing and talking opened up a wellspring of anger, and the Party—insisting on its continued right to a monopoly of power, clinging to its exculpatory version of the past—became its exclusive target.

The system that depended on the enthusiasm and credulity of the masses to move mountains can be mimicked today but not restored. Thousands of people are in jail, but millions in Beijing and all over the country, including Party members and officials, participated in or sympathized with the demonstrations. The job of punishing nonconformists has again been assigned to the Party secretaries of the work units. But their bargain with their subordinates is to live and let live. The central departments order that an editor be fired; his boss orders his retirement but asks him to work as an advisor four days a week. A newspaper reporter comes to cover a meeting held to criticize the "rebellion." After an hour the participants ask him if he has enough for his report, and then they adjourn. Unit members are ordered to criticize one another for something that almost all of them did; an equal black mark is entered in every dossier. Except in jails, repression without popular support has become only ritual.

The Chinese Communist leaders have refused to criticize Mao the way Khrushchev criticized Stalin because they feared the precedent it would set for settling historical accounts. Now they know that their personal accounts will surely be settled, if not before their deaths then after. The closer the reckoning comes the more strongly they resist it. Some in the democracy movement promised a "politics without enemies," but the veteran revolutionaries know this is a myth. The rivals who make up the regime agree not to share power with outsiders; they limit the struggle over power to themselves.

A student leader says that "democracy is a natural desire." It will emerge from the trajectories of 1.2 billion wills. Some people care nothing about politics; they want personal or economic freedom; some are politically desperate, willing to die or even wanting to; some calculate the odds that an act of resistance, small or large, can be carried out without punishment. People watch the signals sent by others. Each calculates the potential cost and gain of resistance, its likelihood of success and risk of failure, and the impact that the same kinds of calculations being made by others might have on their own success. The regime survives on the patience of a people who are waiting for the best time to change it. The unity of the rulers above confronts the patience of the people below. Both conditions are fragile.

Other ruling Communist parties have found their way out of the same impasse by redefining the people who want a voice in their country's future as partners rather than enemies. The CCP may not find this solution, but it will not find another. Most likely, as has happened in Eastern Europe, infirmity in the regime, competition among the leaders, or the determination people see in each other's eyes will signal the crucial moment for a transition to start. But the transition may not be as easy as it has been in Eastern Europe, because the Chinese regime has never depended on an outside army to maintain its hold on power. It has a strong grip and every incentive not to let go.

A liberalizing China will be torn by the same conflicts that have divided it throughout the century: the distribution of wealth between city and rural residents and among different classes, the balance of individual rights with social interests, the roles of government and private enterprise in the economy, the relative authority of the central and provincial governments, and the proper place of the military and the ruling party in a plural society.

How can these issues be resolved within a system of democracy that is workable for China? The same problem faced the reformers who persuaded the emperor at the end of the last century that a democratic system would make the dynasty more stable and prosperous. What such a democracy should be remains unresolved for the Chinese. They must find their own way to square discipline with freedom, social duty with individualism, national goals with personal ones, passion with tolerance, social peace with open conflict, decision with debate. Was it democratic for some students to threaten to burn themselves if the government did not accede to their demands? Was it democratic for intellectuals to try to prevent workers from beating soldiers to death? Was it democratic for some students to refuse to leave the square when a majority wanted to? Who should have spoken for the movement? Who should lead China—a minority of intellectuals who are committed to democracy, or a majority of workers and peasants who may not be? These questions are raised by the reflections on Tiananmen being carried out by Chinese around the world. They follow the hunger-strikers in calling for "the birth of a new political culture."

A Chinese form of democracy will differ from the ideals portrayed in manifestoes and also from the Western models that some Chinese want to emulate. Its prominent features are likely to include a single dominant party descended from the Communists, a fractionated opposition, a turbulent parliament, noisy elections, local political machines, competition for resources among provinces and regions, angry rhetoric, and frequent strikes and demonstrations. This may not be the politics anyone in China wants, but it may result from each Chinese pushing in his or her own way away from the politics China has now. Power that is shared in this way will be diminished, but it may also be more able to gain compliance. Political decisions will become harder to achieve but may be more widely supported. Conflicts will become noiser but easier to identify and deal with. Political leaders will be less secure, but the political system will be more able to adapt and survive.

Mencius said, "If men suddenly see a child about to fall into a well, they will without exception experience a feeling of alarm and distress." China's disasters engage us as human beings because they remind us of how little control we have over our own fates. They involve us as political beings because a China that consumes itself in fruitless struggle deprives us of a partner we need to help solve problems of international security, environmental preservation, and world prosperity. Tiananmen filled us with fear and pity. The making of China's future, however hard and uncertain, will arouse our concern and our hope.

北京市公安局通缉令

各省、自治区直辖市公安厅、局
铁道、交通、民航公安局：

方励之、李淑娴，因犯有反革命宣传煽动
罪畏罪潜逃，北京市公安局已提请市人民检察

POSTSCRIPT

by Fang Lizhi*

The values underlying human dignity are common to all peoples. They are comprised of universally applicable standards of human rights that hold no regard for race, language, religion, or other belief. These universal standards, symbolized by the United Nations Declaration of Human Rights, have increasingly earned the acceptance and respect of the world at large. When a commemorative gathering was held last November in Beijing to honor the fortieth anniversary of the Declaration, many of us were delighted, because it seemed to us at the time that the principles of human rights were finally starting to take root in our ancient land.

However, time after time these fond dreams have been shattered by harsh reality. In the face of the bloody tragedy of last June, we must admit to having been far too optimistic. Some of those who were responsible for this repression have recently attempted to defend their behavior by declaring that "China has its own standards of human rights." They have completely rejected the world's condemnation by refusing to admit the universal nature of human rights. They appear to think that as long as they can dub something a "household affair," to be dealt with internally, they can ignore the laws of human decency and do whatever they please. But this is the worst kind of feudalistic logic. During China's long period of isolation from the rest of the world, this ideology of purporting to be "master of all under heaven" may have been an effective means of controlling the country. But in the latter part of the twentieth century, declarations about "household affairs" only serve to expose those who make them as feudal dictators. Such statements have lost their capacity either to intimidate or deceive.

Nowadays, a growing number of Chinese believe that for China to catch up with the modern world, we must change our own society by absorbing those aspects of more modern civilization that have proven progressive and universal, especially science and democracy. From the movement for science and democracy of 1919 to the rising tide of demand for intellectual freedom of 1957, and from the protest marches of 1926 that were met with swords and guns to the demonstrations of 1989 that were confronted with tanks, we can see how passionately the Chinese people want a just, rational, and prosperous society. Although China has some very deep-seated problems that cause it to lag behind the developed countries, our history clearly shows that the Chinese people have sought the same kind of progress and devel-

opment as people everywhere, no matter their race or nationality. When it comes to such common aspirations, Chinese people are no different from any other. Like all members of the human race, the Chinese are born with a body and a brain, with passions and with a soul. Therefore they can and must enjoy the same inalienable rights, dignity, and liberty as other human beings.

Allow me to draw a historical analogy. Recent propaganda to the effect that "China has its own standards for human rights" bears an uncanny similarity to pronouncements made by our eighteenth-century rulers when they declared that "China has its own astronomy." The feudal aristocracy of 200 years ago opposed the notion of an astronomy based on science. They refused to acknowledge the universal applicability of modern astronomy, or even that it might be of some use in formulating the Chinese calendar. The reason they opposed modern astronomy was that the laws of astronomy, which pertain everywhere, made it quite clear that the "divine right to rule" claimed by these people was a fiction. By the same token, the principles of human rights which also pertain everywhere make it clear that the "right to rule" claimed by some today is just as baseless. This is why rulers from every era, with their special privileges, have opposed the equality inherent in such universal ideas.

The advance of civilization has largely followed from the discovery and development of universally applicable concepts and laws; those who rejected the idea that science applied everywhere were in fact demonstrating their fear of modern civilization. The feudal aristocrats of two centuries past saw astronomy as a bearer of modern culture, and as a result ruthlessly persecuted those engaged in its study and practice. Indeed, in one instance of repression during the early Qing dynasty, five astronomers of the Beijing Observatory were put to death. Far from demonstrating the might of the perpetrators, such brutality only demonstrated their fear. Equally terrified by the implications of universal human rights, modern-day dictators also resort to murder. But no more than in the case of their predecessors should this be construed as an indication of their strength.

Some people say that the terror that has filled Beijing since June can't help but make one feel pessimistic. And I must admit to such feelings of pessimism myself. But I would also like to offer a small bit of encouragement. Remember that in the current climate of terror, it may well be that those who are most terrified are those who have just finished killing their fellow human beings. We may be forced to live under a terror today, but we have no fear of tomorrow. The murderers, on the other hand, are not only fearful today, they are even more terrified of tomorrow. Thus, we have no reason to lose faith. Ignorance may dominate in the short

* Adapted from Fang Lizhi's acceptance speech for the 1989 Robert F. Kennedy Human Rights Award, translated by James H. Williams and Orville Schell.

term through the use of violence, but it will eventually be unable to resist the advance of universal laws. And this will come to pass just as surely as the earth turns.

Of course, it takes time for the earth to turn, and for China things could take even longer. With this in mind, I would like to say a few things to the young Chinese in the audience. I know that many of you have dedicated your lives to building our country anew. Since the road to rebirth will be a long one, I fervently hope that you will not discontinue your education, but instead will work even harder to deepen and enrich your knowledge. We are all disciples of nonviolence. What power can nonviolence summon as a means of resisting the armed violence of guns the world over? There are many strategies of nonviolence, but what is most basic is the force of knowledge. Without knowledge, nonviolence can deteriorate into begging, and history is unmoved by begging. [To paraphrase Einstein] It is only when we stand on the shoulders of the giant of knowledge that we will truly be able to change the course of history. Only with knowledge will we be able to overcome the violence of ignorance at its very roots. Only with knowledge will we have the compassion necessary to deliver from their folly those with superstitious faith in the omnipotence of violence. As Ibsen said, "If you want to be of value to society, there is no better way than to forge yourself into a vessel for its use." I hope that all of us will strive to forge ourselves into such vessels.

Many friends have expressed great concern about my current situation, and from the bottom of our hearts my wife and I want to take this opportunity to thank both those we already know and those we have not yet met. Because of the extraordinary circumstances under which we now live, I am unable to tell you any of the details of our lives. But there is perhaps one bit of news that may somewhat lighten your hearts. I am doing my best to exercise to their fullest extent two of my remaining rights, namely the right to think and the right to inquire. I am continuing my research in astrophysics, and since June of this year I have already written two research papers and am now in the midst of a third.

In the field of modern cosmology, the first principle is called "the Cosmological Principle." It says that the universe has no center, that it has the same properties throughout. Every place in the universe has, in this sense, equal rights. How can the human race, which has evolved in a universe of such fundamental equality, fail to strive for a society without violence and terror? How can we fail to build a world in which the rights due to every human being from birth are respected?

May the blessings of the universe be upon us all.

My thanks to everyone.

Deng Xiaoping and members
of the martial-law troops.
Wu Jingsheng (Xinhua)

ACKNOWLEDGMENTS

After the tragic events of June 1989, a group of Chinese scientists studying in this country came up with the idea that eventually evolved into this book. Creating a book, however, is a massive undertaking. Photographs had to be gathered, interviews conducted, and articles translated and edited. The final product is the result of the hard work and dedication of many people.

Aryeh Neier, Sidney Jones, Kenneth Roth, Robin Munro, Carol Drake, Jeannine Guthrie, and the staff of Asia Watch and Human Rights Watch provided invaluable support and assistance throughout the production of the book.

John K. Fairbank, Orville Schell, Jonathan Spence, Andrew J. Nathan, and Perry Link donated their writings and contributed valuable expertise and advice as the project developed.

A special thanks is owed to the executive photographic editor and book designer, Robert Pledge. He was aided by two associate art directors: Zohra Mokhtari, who executed the layout; and Mark Rykoff, who handled general editorial coordination and production. Many others helped with the initial selection of photographs: Jocelyne Benzakin, Howard Chapnick, Robert Dannin, Laurence Derimay, Caroline Lachowsky, Eliane Laffont, Fred Ritchin, Mary Shea, Claude Terce, and Shi Zhimin. Claude Maggiori and Michael Rand provided useful suggestions on the general design. The staff of Contact Press Images rendered invaluable services.

In addition to Contact Press Images, Associated Press/Wide World Photos, Black Star Publishing Company, Detroit Free Press, Magnum Photos, JB Pictures, Sygma and Vu provided a large portion of the photographs, all of which were donated. Gamma, the H. K. Lau Collection, Impact Photos, K & W, Photo Shuttle: Japan, Reuters-Bettmann Archive, Select, Sovfoto and many individual photographers also generously contributed material free of charge.

Senior editor Fergus M. Bordewich, associate editor Ellen Goldberg, and others provided editorial support: David Seto, Anthony Yang, Li Ming, James Huang, Lan Yishen, Tracy Jones, Joy Chen, as well as our freelance editors, Susanne Wah Lee and Mitch Berman. We would also like to thank our editors at Macmillan, John Glusman and Robert Kimzey, as well as our production manager, Twisne Fan; design director, Janet Tingey; production editor, Tony Davis; and copyeditor, Jane Herman.

We would like to thank all the photographers, Abbas, Ah Jiao, Shunsuke Akatsuka, Mark Avery, Hei Bai, David Neil Berkwitz, Rene Burri, Henri Cartier-Bresson, Peter Charlesworth, Davy, Fang Mu, Stuart Franklin, Gabriel, Sydney Gamble, Greg Girard, Garrige Ho, Koichi Imaeda, Kenneth Jarecke, Jacques Langevin, Erica Lansner, Li Jin, Liu Heung Shing, Luo Xiaoyun, Dario Mitidieri, Hiroshi Nakanishi, Rei Ohara, Atsuko Otsuka, Gabriela Medina P., Alon Reininger, Fred Scott, Ta Hsiuhsien, David C. Turnley, Peter Turnley, Manuel Vimenet, Peter Wang, Jeff Widener, Ken Wong, Wu Jingsheng, Wu Yue, Patrick Zachmann, and Zong Hoi Yi.

CCBA, Jack-Hsieh Memorial Foundation, M. B. Lee, Robin Radin, Yan Guoji, other artists, and many friends of Human Rights in China provided generous financial support.

The Parisian photo lab Pictorial Service, as well as the TIME/LIFE Photo Lab, Loy-Taubman Color Lab Inc. and Aurora Color Lab Inc. in New York provided us with flawless photographic services at a significant discount.

Ding Xueliang conducted many interviews.

We would especially like to thank all those who gave us interviews.

Roland Algrant, Ai Weiwei, Tom Bettag, Cathy Bostron, Kay Cheung, Andrew Chiang, Lynn Chu, E. L. Doctorow, Glenn Hartley, Erica Lansner, Sarah

Lazin, Tom Grunfeld, Dan Rather, Ruan Ming, Harrison Salisbury, Shi Tianjian, Sun Jinyu, and James Tu offered valuable advice.

Suzanne Fox, John Gardner, Andrew Joseph, Han Jining, Li Luyuan, Pei Minxin, Tang Sanyee, and H. Y. Wang helped with translation of the text.

Joan Judge, Andrea Worden, Philip Cunningham, Carol Benedict, Ellen Laing, Wayne Xing, and Dana Wolf conducted a great deal of research.

United Daily News, China Spring, Pei Shen magazine, South China Morning Post, and Mr. Wu Moren granted us permission to quote from their publications. And we thank Fang Mu, Cheng Yu for making their articles available.

Many other individuals and organizations gave generously of their time and talent in every phase of production: Hilary Beattie, Beiling, Doris Brautigan, Gail Butler, Kathy Charlton, Alex Chen, Chen Hsinyuan, Sam Chen, Oscar Chiang, Martia Cohen, Catherine G. Curran, Carlo De Vito, Seth Faison, John Fei, Fu Zhengyuan, Andrea Gambino, Daniel Gastel, Gregory Headberg, Jim Herschberg, Michael Hickman, T. C. Hsu, Hu Xiaomin, Dede Huang, Judy Inn, Yuan Jiang, H. Kwan Lau, Sharon Lee, S. E. Levinston, Li Mo, David Leung, the New York Academy of Arts, the Chinese Language Journalists' Association, Philippe Marinig, Christine Normoyle, Michelle Osterfeld, Andrew Page, Neil Peng, Stuart Pivar, Jake Prescott, John Pritchard, Qi Lan, John Rong, Aaron Schindler, Michel Sixou, Judy Smith, Tom Smith, Norman Snyder, Hal Stucker, Su Hsong-Hsien, Lawrence R. Sullivan, Eva Tan, Eric Taubman, Freda Wang, Joan Worden, Wu Zhongcao, Lily Yeh, Zhang Baoluo, Zhang Hongtu, Zhang Shiping, as well as those who, to protect their families in China, must remain anonymous.

And finally, the commitment and dedication of many members of Human Rights in China were essential to the publication of this book. They are: Cheng Ye, Tang Sanyee, Han Jining, Li Luyuan, Pei Minxin, Kay Cheung, Feng Qun, Xie Zuqi, Wu Weishi, Chen Longyin, Chen Reimin, Ding Hongqiang, Fei Dongyu, Hu Xiaoming, Lan Yishen, Li Shaomin, Li Xiaorong, Lin Yinlian, Liu Xianfang, Lu Jianping, Ma Bo, Ma Jun, Pan Zhaoxin, Shao Zhifeng, Shen Zhiyong, Shi Tianjian, Wang Shiqing, Yang Qinyun, Yang Yubo, Yuan Xiaoping, Yang Zhi, Zhang Yuanchong, Zhang Zenghui, Zhang Zheng, Zhou Renping, and Zhou Zhou.

Xin-Yuan Fu, Ph.D
Director
Human Rights in China, Inc.

Peter Wang
Managing Editor
Children of the Dragon

Stuart Franklin (Magnum)